I have often said that there are two passions in my spirit. One is for the unity of the body. The other is a passion for God's presence. This is a "presence" book. Dale Fife writes eloquently and experientially of God's presence. You can almost smell the smoke of the incense from inside the Holy Place when you read this.

—Tommy Tenney,
Author of *The God Chasers*

I have walked with the Lord long enough to know when I am having an encounter with Him—in worship, intercession, in the Scriptures, in the writings of Oswald Chambers, and now, for sure, in Dale's book. I was touched at the very core of my being, and I sensed an immediate longing to get to my own "Secret Place."

—Bishop Joseph Garlington,
Senior Pastor, Author, Recording Artist,
Covenant Church of Pittsburgh, Pittsburgh, PA

Every now and then a book comes along that is life-changing. *The Secret Place* is just such a book. Get ready for an incredible journey into the presence of the living God. Prepare yourself to touch the Father's heart. Within these pages you will experience a depth of prophetic revelation and insight that will provoke you to respond to God's invitation to intimacy. I encourage you to read this book and to recommend it to others. It will inspire, instruct, and challenge you. Thank you, Dale, for opening the well of prophetic revelation and drawing up incredible insight from the depths of God's wisdom.

—Mark Chironna,
Senior Pastor, Author, and TV Host on TBN,
Mark Chironna Ministries, Orlando, FL

A yearning for the presence of God has become increasingly more evident throughout the body of Christ. A timely response to the inner cry of believers everywhere is Dale Fife's work, *The Secret Place*. This wonderful book vividly captures the essence of communion between God and man. If you long to experience a greater intimacy with the Father, I highly recommend this book. Your heart will be stirred to seek the face of God, page after page!

—Dr. Kingsley A. Fletcher,
Senior Pastor, Author, International Speaker,
Life Community Church, Raleigh, NC

What a treat to draw from the rich revelation of *The Secret Place*. Read and devour! Dale's experience with God created a hunger, a holy appetite in me for that "deeper relationship" that only He can satiate. Accept this prophetic invitation to intimacy with God. Taste and see that the Lord is good!

—Rev. Jill Griffith,
Teacher, Author, Conference Speaker,
Kingdom Connections International, Inc., Houston, TX

It is very clear to me that believers across the globe are experiencing the passionate call to encounter God's presence. The result is a people passionately in love with Christ, ready to build the local church and extend the kingdom of God. As you read Dale's book, *The Secret Place,* the Holy Spirit will bring a powerful, supernatural encounter, which in turn will catapult you into a whole new lifestyle and dedication to Jesus. Read this book and change history!

—Adrian Gray,
Senior Pastor,
Mount Annan Church, Sydney, Australia

As you open the pages of this book, you had better be prepared to take a journey that will lead you into new dimensions of spiritual truth and experience. This journey is open to all who are hungry and thirsty for greater reality, who seek substance over symbolism, reality above rhetoric, and the fire of passion over the slough of mediocrity. Dale will lead you past the ankle-deep water into the deeper waters of the Spirit. Thank you, Dale, for your contribution to the great work our Lord Jesus is doing in these days.

—Don Milam,
Author,
Shippensburg, PA

A book that results from personal intimacy with God is far more inspiring than one that is a product of speculation. Dr. Dale Fife is an individual who has dedicated himself to exploring the hidden realities of Christian experience through prayer. During my frequent visits to his pastorate in Farmington, Connecticut, and through his anointed ministry in our Bible college, I have found him to be well equipped and qualified to write this exciting book. *The Secret Place* is an authentic call from the throne room of heaven to which all of us need to respond. The readers of this book will be greatly rewarded in their spiritual thirst for God by discovering the joy of abundant life in His presence.

—Dr. John Thannickal,
President, New Life College,
Bangalore, India

THE SECRET PLACE

Passionately Pursuing His Presence

THE SECRET PLACE

Passionately Pursuing His Presence

DR. DALE A. FIFE

WHITAKER
HOUSE

THE SECRET PLACE

For speaking engagements, you may contact the author at:
Dr. Dale A. Fife
The Potter's House
326 Brickyard Road
Farmington, CT 06032
e-mail: MnTopMin@aol.com

ISBN: 0-88368-715-1
Printed in the United States of America
© 2001 by Dr. D. Arthur Fife

Whitaker House
30 Hunt Valley Circle
New Kensington, PA 15068
www.whitakerhouse.com

Library of Congress Cataloging-in-Publication Data

Fife, D. Arthur (Dale Arthur), 1942–
The secret place : a prophetic invitation to intimacy with God / by D. Arthur Fife.
p.   cm.
Includes bibliographical references.
ISBN 0-88368-715-1 (pbk. : alk. paper)
1. Private revelations.   I. Title.
BV5091.R4 F54 2001
248.2'9—dc21
2001005383

4 5 6 7 8 9 10 11 12 13 14 ∿ 11 10 09 08 07 06 05 04 03

This book is lovingly dedicated to my wonderful wife,
Eunice Arline Fife.
Her pure heart, her love for God, and her constant affection and
encouragement are priceless treasures to me.

Contents

Foreword

etrospect is that marvelous faculty whereby we are enabled to gaze with wisdom upon a series of events to which we were totally oblivious when they occurred. We can now view these with a learned look upon our faces, as if we "knew it all the time." Whenever we come to understand a paradox that formerly mystified us, things suddenly make sense. Those former mysteries become the basic building blocks that lead to even greater discoveries.

I have known Dale Fife for more than twenty-seven years, and after reading *The Secret Place,* I'm finally beginning to understand the paradox that Dale Fife is. When others are simply looking at something, he is seeing the same thing, but in a fresh new way. When I read his manuscript, I revisited feelings I had when I first read C. S. Lewis's *Out of the Silent Planet.* Lewis's capacity to capture in words and communicate deep spiritual truths is what drew me to his writings. Dale's gift is strangely similar, and as we read his words, we are irresistibly drawn into a world that exists right alongside the world we are so preoccupied with every day. He draws upon universally recognized symbols that touch in us what some would call "the collective unconscious," or what Solomon called *"eternity in their heart"* (Eccl. 3:11).

My initial intention was to "scan" this book for a dear friend who asked me to read it and share my thoughts. After a few moments, however,

I was joining him on this glorious adventure in intimate prayer. Although my experience was vicarious, time seemed to stand still. The imagery he used to describe his experiences in *The Secret Place* was strangely compelling. I have walked with the Lord long enough to know when I am having an encounter with Him—in worship, intercession, in the Scriptures, in the writings of Oswald Chambers, and now, for sure, in Dale's book. I was touched at the very core of my being, and I sensed an immediate longing to get to my own "Secret Place."

When I first met Dale, he was leading a very successful weekly gathering of youth and young adults. Along with many other pastors and leaders in western Pennsylvania, he had been introduced to the Holy Spirit in a deeper way, and that experience had greatly impacted his life and ministry. In addition to pastoring a traditional denominational church, he gathered on a weekly basis hundreds of young people in a barn in suburban Pittsburgh, Pennsylvania. These kids were on fire, and the meetings were alive with the presence of God. Dale had a deep passion for worship, a solid gift as a musician, an infectious sense of humor, and remarkable insights into the Scriptures that captivated both his youthful and mature audiences. These attributes were a winning combination with these Spirit-hungry kids, and attendance at the meetings multiplied rapidly.

The enthusiasm was not shared, however, by the local leadership of his church. There were grumblings about the new direction the church was taking, and there was a significant measure of dissatisfaction with all this Holy Spirit "stuff." Some people were complaining because of the changes that were quickly taking place, and resistance to those changes began to steadily grow. These new concepts seemed to be a radical departure from their authentic historic expression, and therefore needed to be curbed. Now, what seemed to be a God-given answer to drawing young people into the church became a threat to those wanting to maintain the status quo. This newly revived pastor was awakened to a new reality: our church doesn't want this new life! It was now apparent that there was real pressure being applied by some of his denominational leaders to "rein him in." It seemed that some of those leaders believed that this was not an authentic expression of their historic church. (They were wrong, of course.)

It was in this milieu that an ultimatum was given. The leadership decided that the ministry at the barn was not sanctioned, and that any potential for Dale's advancement in the church would depend upon his willingness to return to a more conservative approach to ministry. He realized that he was being asked to back away from his newfound commitment to the life and work of the Holy Spirit in his church and ministry. He was seeing more fruit in his ministry than he had ever seen. He was stunned by the demand to walk away and not "ruin" his ministry career. It was in this season that *the dream* came.

Dr. John Guest, a prominent pastor and evangelist, defines the word *kairos* as "a critical moment in time by which history is changed." Dale experienced his personal *kairos* after he had a certain dream. I can still recall the profound look on Dale's countenance when he shared his dream with me. He had been wrestling with the decision to stay at the church and virtually abandon the exciting road he was now traveling, or to leave everything he had worked for up to that time—friends, coworkers, and even family. In the midst of these troubling events, he had a dream that catalyzed his decision to leave. In the dream, he was asleep and suddenly awakened by the screams of a huge bird of prey descending upon his exposed chest with talons drawn. He cried out, and the creature left. Upon awakening, he was visibly shaken and wondered at the meaning.

Several days later, he happened to be at a friend's home where the Bible just "happened" to be lying open on the coffee table to Psalm 74:19, which reads, *"Give not to the vulture, the life of your dove."* This translation, from the *New American Bible,* is the only one in which this verse is rendered in these exact words. In one incredible moment, the dream (the subjective) and the Scripture (the objective) came together with the kind of power that you experience only with that sure knowledge that God is speaking directly to you.

When Dale shared his dream with me, I had a feeling that comes on rare occasions. There are some experiences in life that, when shared, have such a deep and universal meaning that the hearer realizes in utter amazement: "I know that dream!" The psalmist said, *"Deep calls to deep"* (Ps. 42:7), and when one person touches the deep place in another, he touches that eternal deposit that resides in the heart of every man. Over the years of our friendship and partnership in ministry, Dale has had the capacity to do this on innumerable occasions in my life, and in the lives of thousands of others who have drunk from his streams. That "big" dream, when knitted together with the passage in the Psalms, provided the answer and the assurance he was desperately seeking.

I also believe that Dale's *kairos* became the matrix that nurtured in him a deeper desire for intimacy and propelled him irresistibly toward his life's call: to "see" the invisible things of God's purpose and to credibly communicate them to those who cannot initially see *"unless someone guides* [them]" (Acts 8:31). In *The Secret Place*, Dale's call has come to fruition. Moses told the children of Israel, *"The secret things belong to the LORD our God, but the things revealed belong to us and to our sons forever, that we may observe all the words of this law"* (Deut. 29:29). Solomon said, *"It is the glory of God to conceal a matter, but the glory of kings is to search out a matter"* (Prov. 25:2).

Reading this book is at first very similar to trying to find your way around an unfamiliar and darkened room. You will grope, and you will bump into things until your eyes become accustomed to the new environment. As you begin to master your surroundings, you will begin to "see" things that have always been there. If, however, you have spent more time stimulating your imagination through television and movies, you will need some time to become accustomed to this strange new world of intimacy. In this world, the language is of the heart; and that language is primarily pictorial and filled with imagery, much like dreams and visions.

If you lack a basic familiarity with the Scriptures, you will struggle to grasp the deep yet simple truths toward which my friend is guiding you. I urge you, however, to trust him; he will be a faithful guide. He has been a disciplined student of the Word for more than three decades. Expect to "see" some things you've never seen and to visit some places that may be new to you but are very familiar to many of the saints through the centuries of church history. With a competent guide, one can travel a mere hour from one's primary residence and discover a whole new world!

This is also true with the Scriptures and prayer; they may be unfamiliar, because they're not places that the average Christian frequently visits. Nevertheless, your ultimate destination is not a place, but a Person. The journey you will take in these pages—if you persevere—will lead you to the face of the One who is summoning you to Himself through these powerful images. Paul told the Corinthians, *"Now we see through a glass, darkly; but then face to face"* (1 Cor. 13:12 KJV).

It is my hope that *The Secret Place* will awaken a hunger in all the Father's children for a deeper and richer fellowship with Him. It is my prayer that this clarion call to intimacy with God will touch the heart-strings of every seeking believer. It is my conviction that few will remain the same when they have finished the journey through these pages. It is my belief that my friend has unselfishly shared a truly remarkable encounter with the triune God; and the gifts of writing and language, which He bestowed upon him, are graciously evident in these pages. May the Holy Spirit, who inspired these words, stir each of us to pursue our own adventure in *The Secret Place.*

—Bishop Joseph L. Garlington,
Senior Pastor, Covenant Church of Pittsburgh,
President, Reconciliation! An International Network of Churches and
Ministries, Inc.

Preface

This book is the result of my burning passion for intimacy with the Lord. One day I simply said to the Lord that I wanted to be like Enoch. I wanted to be His friend and to walk daily with Him. He not only heard my prayer, but also answered it! That day and that prayer have changed my life forever. These pages are the actual account of what I experienced because of my request.

The open vision, beginning in the second part of the book, was not a single event, but rather a process that continued over a period of weeks. It culminated in such intense intimacy with God that, at times, I was so overcome with emotion and the overwhelming awareness of His awesome presence, I could hardly write in my journal what He was showing me. Tears flooded my eyes and streaked down my cheeks. There were moments of such intense physical heat, I thought that my body would be consumed. The weight of His glory demanded that I bow my head in reverence.

My daily walks with the Lord began with the simple act of quietly waiting in His presence. On some occasions, I felt strongly impressed to pray in the Spirit. After several moments of prayer, the Lord would make His presence known, and we would resume our journey of revelation together. Thus, He progressively led me further into the mysteries of His purpose and revealed Himself to me through visions.

The people I encountered on this journey were as real to me as my family and friends. You no doubt recognize some of their names. Others are heavenly creatures or angels with identifiable characteristics and personalities.

I took great caution never to impose my thoughts or opinions upon the vision the Lord was showing me. There were moments of apprehension and fear, when I realized the great danger of doing so. Day after day, God graciously confirmed the truth of the revelation through the Scriptures. He was speaking to me! He really was drawing close to me, and out of this intimacy, He was revealing His heart *to me*.

I can certainly identify with Paul the apostle when he wrote to the Corinthian Christians,

> *Boasting is necessary, though it is not profitable; but I will go on to visions and revelations of the Lord. I know a man in Christ who fourteen years ago—whether in the body I do not know, or out of the body I do not know, God knows—such a man was caught up to the third heaven. And I know how such a man—whether in the body or apart from the body I do not know, God knows—was caught up into Paradise, and heard inexpressible words, which a man is not permitted to speak. On behalf of such a man will I boast; but on my own behalf I will not boast, except in regard to my weaknesses. For if I do wish to boast I shall not be foolish, for I shall be speaking the truth; but I refrain from this, so that no one may credit me with more than he sees in me or hears from me.*
> (2 Cor. 12:1–6)

I gladly acknowledge my weaknesses. I claim no special inspiration. My sole desire is to be faithful to the Lord Jesus Christ and His Word. Without apology, I hold fast to the inerrancy and infallible inspiration of the Holy Scriptures. The Bible is the only absolute standard by which this, and all prophetic revelation, must be tested and judged (2 Tim. 3:16–17; 2 Pet. 1:19–21).

It is my sincere prayer that those who read this compendium of dreams, visions, Scripture, prayer, prophecy, and journaling will discern that it weaves an incredible tapestry of revelation from the heart of God for His church. These are spiritual words, intended for spiritual people. (See I Corinthians 2:6–16.) Let him who has spiritual ears hear what the Spirit is saying to the church in these days.

There are several dramatic changes in my personal life and relationship with the Lord as a result of this intense time of intimacy with God. One of the greatest consequences is a new, and very acute, awareness of the absolute reality of the spiritual world, the heavenly realm, and angelic beings. I can honestly say that, at times, the spiritual world is more real to me than the physical. The term *supernatural* has taken on a whole new significance.

Finally, I want to say that I will never again be satisfied with a life that lacks intimacy with the living God. If someday I start off walking with Him and don't return from that walk, you will know that I have followed in Enoch's footsteps. Realize that I just couldn't bear the thought of leaving God's presence again.

To everyone who longs for this kind of intimacy with God, I can attest to the fact that He is more desirous of intimacy with you than you are with Him. Even when I feared that He might not be waiting to speak to me or would cease to walk with me in sweet fellowship, He never disappointed me. Not only was I never disappointed, but, more often than not, when I would miss a day or two of communion with Him, He would always express His sadness that I didn't come into His presence sooner. He was waiting for me all along.

To all who hunger and thirst for intimacy with the living God, He is waiting for you to draw near!

Acknowledgments

I am deeply indebted to the modern-day, Holy Spirit-led prophets and Christians who have cleared an authentic biblical path of prophetic insight through the dark forest of New Age confusion and Eastern mysticism pervading our time. Their willingness to share what they have learned with the wider church, sometimes at great sacrifice, has helped me to achieve a place of intimacy with the Lord, which I believe would have been unattainable without their guidance and instruction. Their courage and obedience to the Holy Spirit are an example for us to emulate.

The longing of contemporary Christians is an echo of the same heart-cry that our spiritual fathers and mothers expressed when they sought the solitude of the desert in order to hear God's voice during the infancy of the church. The medieval monasteries and convents still serve as a repository of wisdom for those who long for singleness of heart. Brother Lawrence, Saint Teresa of Avila, Michael Molinos, Saint John of the Cross, and Madame Guyon are only a few of the saints who pressed past the mediocrity of religion with impassioned hearts to seek His face. The modern-day expression of passion and hunger for intimacy with God, exemplified by Evelyn Underhill, Thomas Merton, and most recently men like Tommy Tenney, are part and parcel of the ancient cry to know God and plumb the depths of His mysteries.

God instructed the prophet Jeremiah to *"write all the words which I have spoken to you in a book"* (Jer. 30:2). I have diligently sought to record and interpret what the Lord has spoken to me. The following individuals, in particular, have helped me to develop a hearing ear.

Bishop Joseph Garlington, my spiritual father, mentor, and friend in the Lord, was the first to encourage me to pay closer attention to my dreams. He directed me to the writings of men like Herman Riffel, Morten Kelsey, and Mark Virkler. These authors opened my eyes to the deeper reality of the spiritual world.

In recent decades, the ministry of the prophet has been dynamically restored to the church. Mark Chironna, James Erb, Sharon Stone, and Gary Brooks have personally impacted my life. Their personal ministry and teaching, along with a multitude of other internationally recognized prophetic ministers, have helped me to tap into the Spirit of prophecy and activate the prophetic gift in my own life.

There is one special person who has blessed my life beyond measure: my wife, Eunice. She has constantly encouraged me to seek the Lord. Her diligent prayers have often ushered me into His holy presence. Her joy of seeing me walk with God and hear His voice is one of the greatest rewards I could receive.

"[My inheritance has] *fallen to me in pleasant places"* (Ps. 16:6). To the congregation and leadership of The Potter's House in Farmington, Connecticut, and all of my colleagues and friends in ministry, thank you for being a constant source of blessing and encouragement for me to seek His face.

But you, when you pray, go into your inner room, and when you have shut your door, pray to your Father who is in secret, and your Father who sees in secret will repay you.
—Matthew 6:6

Part One

Dreams and Visions

Chapter One

In the Spirit
I Can Fly

The last golden rays of the late evening sun filtered through the trees, casting long shadows on the pond near the road leading to the geodesic dome. People were just beginning to arrive at the church for the Friday evening Watch Night prayer gathering. They lingered outside to chat with friends, enjoying the few remaining minutes of daylight. Finally, they made their way into the circular auditorium. There was a sense of excitement and anticipation in the air. They actually looked happy. Everyone was thrilled to be there. Could these be Christians coming to a prayer meeting? What was so different about this gathering?

Prayer meetings at The Potter's House were taking on a whole new dimension as a fresh revelation of intercessory prayer exploded into the body of Christ at large and began to impact our local church. Attending the prayer and spiritual warfare conferences being held in the United States and Canada had revitalized several of our people. The resulting spiritual renewal was releasing new freedom, joy, and healing into our congregation.

Prayer Is Exciting

Prayer was actually becoming exciting! For many of us, it was the highlight of the week. God was teaching us how to pray. Our plan was to begin at 7:30 and to stay as long as necessary in order to complete our prayer assignments from the Lord. We felt like spiritual soldiers reporting for duty. We were waiting for our Commander to give us our orders regarding what to pray for.

The meeting began with enthusiastic, vibrant worship. Children and adults circled the auditorium and moved up and down the aisles, waving streamers and flags in praise to the Lord Jesus. Others stood, with their hands raised in adoration, pouring out expressions of worship to the King of Kings and Lord of Lords. There were no spectators in this group. Everyone had come to be in His presence and to seek His face.

After more than thirty minutes of spontaneous worship and praise, we gathered at the front of the auditorium. People were seated in chairs or on the platform steps. Some had spread their Bibles and notepads on the floor where they were reclining. The younger children lay on blankets at the sides of the auditorium, surrounded by stuffed animals and toys. A few of them had already nodded off to sleep. We were a casual bunch of believers, with no religious constraints or time parameters. Our single purpose was to seek the Lord together and to hear Him speak to us what was on His heart.

One of the leading intercessors gave a short teaching on how important it is to cleanse our thoughts and our lives before we enter into intercessory prayer. We spent some time allowing the Holy Spirit to search our hearts. This precipitated a period of personal confession and repentance. Then we waited quietly in His presence.

Surrender Your Options

My eyes were closed as I sat on the second step of the platform. The presence of God became increasingly evident. Suddenly, without any effort or prompting on my part, I saw in my mind drops of water falling into a large pool. It was like having a dream, yet I knew I was awake. In the vision, ripples began to form in the pool and move outward in every direction. The Spirit impressed upon me that these ripples represented God's power. He wanted to release His power from this small gathering of intercessors. That supernatural power would go far beyond this building.

"O God," I prayed, "we long for intimacy with You. We give You this time, Lord. We are Yours to use as instruments of prayer."

His response came instantly. "Will you surrender your *options* to Me?" He asked.

I was stunned by His question. My heart was laid bare by His words. I thought I had kept this issue a well-hidden secret. Only my wife knew about my personal agenda and future plans. I was immediately convicted. There were two options in my life that I had been unwilling to surrender to Him.

The first option that I had reserved was my right to leave the ministry and to walk away from serving Him if things got too tough. The second option I had held on to was my freedom to choose to leave New England. The spiritual ground here in the Northeast was very difficult to plow. Over the years, many pastors had given up and left. I was very discouraged and disheartened myself. My ten years of spiritual labor had reaped so little fruit for my efforts.

Will you surrender entirely to God?

I had reserved the right to determine my own future instead of letting Him decide. I had even gone so far as making elaborate plans to move south. I had spent hours thinking about how to escape the assignment He had given me in Connecticut. The prospect of living a life free from the cares and pressures of ministry was very tempting to me.

Then I heard Him say, "Son, you really have no options except obedience or disobedience."

Suddenly, I realized how foolish I had been. How deceived my thinking was! In that moment, I surrendered my right to leave the ministry and abandon my assignment in New England. Immediately, I felt a deep sense of relief settle into my soul. Peace entered into my spirit as I let go of my security blanket. I was finally free! It was now a settled issue.

The Lord had known all along about these hidden issues in my life. Like all His children, I was in His sovereign process of spiritual growth.

Obedience brings blessing and rest.

His desire was to release me into greater fruitfulness in His service, but it required my complete surrender to His will. He intended it for my good. I finally had the assurance that I could trust Him with my future. I knew I had made the right choice. Obedience is the place of blessing and rest.

On Angels' Wings

I changed my position and moved to the top of the platform. As I lifted my hands in worship and surrender to the Lord, the Holy Spirit began to speak powerfully again through a second vision. In the opening scene, I was aware of four angels hovering over me. One of them spoke to me in the Spirit.

"Do you want to go with us?" he said, looking directly into my eyes. With an expression of hopefulness, he paused to await my response.

I knew intuitively that these angels had come to take me on a spiritual journey somewhere.[1] I felt no fear or hesitancy to accept their invitation.

"Yes, I want to go with you," my heart responded.

The four angels covered me with their wings, and I felt myself being lifted up in the Spirit through the ceiling of the church. We hovered above the building, suspended in the dark night sky. One of the angels pointed toward a building nearby. I had an immediate sense that there was a great evil residing there. A foreboding blackness seemed to pervade the very structure. The angels were warning me of something. Whatever it was, I knew that it was a spiritual force affecting our entire community. Even though I did not understand it entirely, I sensed that I needed to pray about it and that God was strategically showing me how to pray.

Then we ascended far above the earth. I could see a huge line of light moving toward our planet. It filled the heavens as far as I could see. As the line approached, I realized that it was made up of powerful white horses and golden chariots blazing like fire. They were poised for attack. They were being held back, kept from charging ahead toward the earth. The Lord Himself was restraining them. I heard a voice saying, "Tell the church! Warn the church!" I felt it was symbolic of God's pending judgment and the need for the church to wake up and pray.

When I looked back toward the earth, I saw smoke rising from over Europe, like a nuclear cloud. It was so large that it covered the entire continent. It was as if a terrible war had come upon the land. I sensed that God was reinforcing the urgency of prayer for all the nations. I was beginning to see that intercessory prayer can go beyond your own community and make a significant impact on the entire earth.

The next thing I knew, in my spirit I was in the middle of Russia. I was descending toward a Russian house. As I entered the home, I could see a child lying in a bed in the living room. The room was brightly lit and nicely furnished. It had a warm family feel about it. The child was very ill and was about to die. I knew intuitively that I had been enlisted to pray for this little boy. I felt such love and compassion for him. I approached the bed, laid my hands upon the child, and began to pray. The power of God surged through my body. Instantly, I knew that the child was healed.

The scene in the vision immediately changed. I saw myself in an old European city, walking down a cobblestone street that was illuminated by lantern-shaped, wrought-iron streetlights on metal poles. My spiritual journey had led me to a place with an old-world atmosphere about it. The dimly lit streets glistened with reflections of flickering lamps on the shiny cobblestones that had been recently moistened by rainfall. The sidewalk was deserted, and the multistoried houses that lined both sides of the street were all darkened.

As I walked along the street, I came to an alley. Turning the corner, my eyes fell upon a horrible scene. There, lying in the filthy alley, was a beautiful woman. She had been crying out for help, but no one had come to her aid. She had been raped and beaten violently, and she was bleeding profusely. She wore a white dress that was now torn and soiled by large red stains from her own blood.

Recovering from my shock at the horror of the sight, I bent down, picked her up in my arms, and carried her from the dark alley. My heart was broken for her. Her innocence and virginity had been violently taken from her. I felt the anger of God rise up within me. I held her tightly, gently comforting her, and I prayed that no bitterness or poison would destroy her because of this horrible experience.

> *Intercession connects the living power of God with the world.*

The scene faded, and I suddenly found myself somewhere over the Atlantic Ocean, engulfed in the midst of a ferocious storm. The waves were gigantic! The wind was blowing with such force that it drove the rain in massive horizontal sheets, like projectiles fired from many guns. In the midst of this tempest, I could see a sailing yacht being tossed by the huge swells. A wave that towered over the tiny vessel was approaching. I realized that the yacht was about to be capsized. I rushed toward it and placed both of my hands upon the side of the yacht, in the midsection, to stabilize it. I held my position as the massive wave struck the helpless vessel with a thunderous roar. Miraculously, it remained upright!

I breathed a sigh of relief, and, glancing to my right, I noticed a glow of light at the bow of the craft. I was delighted to discover that it emanated from invisible angels who were stationed there. Then I noticed this same glow surrounding the entire vessel. Immediately I realized that the occupants of the yacht had been desperately crying out to the Lord to come and save them. God had enlisted me to intercede for their deliverance from the terrible storm. Their prayers had been answered! Then the Lord revealed to me that the couple aboard the yacht had several young children at home in America. He was planning to use these children mightily for His work. God moves on behalf of His people, and this family, like all His children, was very important to Him.

The vision instantly vanished, and I was aware of my church surroundings again. I had no idea how long I had been praying. I was totally unaware of what had transpired with the others who were in the meeting. They were probably wondering what was happening to me. I knew only that I had been on a journey of prayer in the Spirit. The vision of each place was so real to me that I could describe them in great detail. The emotions I felt during this prayer journey were so acute; it was as if I had actually experienced each event and scene. The sick child; the bleeding, brokenhearted woman; and the distressed couple who were about to drown in the stormy sea were all real people to me. They all had cried out to God in desperation. Their pleas for help had come up before Him, and He had enlisted me as an intercessor in response to their prayers.

I was taken up in the Spirit and escorted by angelic beings on a prayer journey. I had traveled to places I had never been in the flesh in order to intercede for people whom I had never met, all because they had prayed and cried out to God. I was an intercessor on assignment, and in the Spirit I could fly.

Intercessory prayer would never be the same for me again. Through this incredible experience, the Lord taught me that intercession is much more than coming before Him with a checklist of needs and requests. Instead, it is reporting for duty, allowing Him to search our hearts and cleanse us, and then letting Him direct our prayer focus as we wait before Him.

Ripples of Prayer Power

The vision of the ripples in the pond, which the Lord had shown me at the beginning of the meeting, now made sense to me. I understood perfectly how a small group of intercessors gathered for prayer could make an incredible difference anywhere in the world if they would simply make themselves available to Him. His power and provision could be dispatched anywhere on the planet at a moment's notice. God is not limited by time or space, and in the Spirit, neither are we!

Chapter Two

Where Is My Passport?

I am an explorer at heart. God must have put it in my genetic code. I remember so well one very special summer day many years ago, when I was only ten years old. Our family seldom went beyond the confines of Pittsburgh, but that particular day was extraordinary. We were headed for Lake Erie for our first entire week of vacation together as a family. We were about to go beyond our boundaries.

I sat by the passenger window on the gray velour rear seat of our Chevrolet sedan. My eyes were wide with excitement as I gazed out upon the passing scenes of city and farmland. I photographed every one of those scenes in my mind. I can still feel the warmth of the morning sun on my face, and the cool sweetness of the country breeze rushing past me from the open front window. The sound of the shifting gears of the standard transmission and the hum of the engine were like music in my ears. I was fully alive! I was going somewhere! My world had suddenly become a place to discover and explore. The thrill and adventure of that first childhood journey has never left me.

Since that first expedition beyond the confines of our neighborhood, I have become a world traveler. What excites me now is the hustle and bustle of an international airport and the smell of jet fuel. Nothing can compare to the surge of unrestrained power as I am pushed into the back of my seat by the thrust of jet engines at full throttle. The raw energy and speed are intoxicating. Instead of viewing the passing landscape from an automobile, now I can peer down from miles above the earth to view a panorama of life and scenery extending from oceans to mountains. Entire cities can be seen in one view.

Japan, India, Brazil, England, Curacao, Jamaica, Mexico, Puerto Rico, Haiti, South Africa, Kenya, Israel, Jordan, Egypt, Australia—these are no longer distant places described in a travel brochure. They are familiar to me because I have been there. I have walked their streets and paths. I have entered homes as simple as a mud hut or as elegant as the Palace of Mysore and the Taj Mahal. I have visited Westminster Cathedral and the Elephanta Caves near Bombay, where people came centuries before Christ to worship stone idols.

I have smelled the intoxicating fragrance of blooming jasmine and danced along the streets of Pretoria covered with the purplish-blue blossoms of the jacaranda trees. From curried chicken to akee with salt fish, I have sampled the cuisine of exotic ports. I have even witnessed the dawn of a new day over the African plains, as the lion and zebra and wildebeest gathered with the giraffe and elephant to drink from the same watering hole in the morning shadows. Dust was already rising from the myriad herds of deer and gazelle as they began their day on the veldt.

A Spiritual Journey

Yes, I love to travel because I am an explorer at heart. But I am curious about more than just the world in which I live. I long to know the God who created it. Like every human being, I am on a spiritual journey of discovery. Instead of pursuing the fountain of youth or some uncharted course to circumnavigate the globe like the early explorers, I am on a much more important quest. I am in pursuit of the living God. I long to draw near to Him.

Every journey ought to begin with thoughtful preparation. Several important questions need to be answered: Where am I going? Why do

I want to go there? What will be needed when I get to my destination? Which clothes are appropriate for the climate? Do I have the necessary equipment and supplies to accomplish my purpose for this particular journey? Of utmost importance is obtaining a valid passport and the appropriate visas that will grant me permission to enter the nations I plan to visit.

While we often ascertain the answers to these questions before setting off on an actual worldwide excursion, we seldom apply these same questions to our spiritual walk. Although the preparation for our journey of faith has been in progress from the very beginning of our lives, more often than not we are unaware of it. Consequently, we fail to ask the Lord where He wants us to be going, and why. Like rudderless ships, we drift *Are you prepared to journey toward intimacy with God?* through life, hoping that we will stumble upon His will and purpose for us.

Some of us clearly hear the call of God and respond in obedience. Like the patriarch Abraham, we realize that God is calling us to get up and leave the comfort of our surroundings and the familiarity of our relatives, and head for a distant place.

Headed toward Intimacy

The Almighty issued Abraham's passport, and along the way He provided safe passage through each stage of the journey. God wants to do the same for us. For Abraham, it was far more than a trip across the landscape to a promised land of abundant provision and blessing. It was a journey of faith that led to intimacy with God. Should it be any less for us modern spiritual travelers?

So we, like Abraham, begin the journey. There is a longing in our hearts that supersedes our obedience to His will. We yearn to find a place of intimacy with Him. We want to see Him face-to-face! We are not content to worship from afar. Instead, we are desperate for His presence. We are more interested in Him than in the destination to which He is leading us. In fact, we discover on our way that He *is* the destination! He is drawing us to Himself, and this is exactly what He intended from the beginning.

It doesn't take us long to realize how inadequate our resources are for this spiritual journey. We are suddenly cast upon His mercy and faithfulness to guide us along the way. At times our spirits are willing, but our flesh is weak, and we are drawn away from Him. The cares of this life and the things of the world entice and seduce us, but He is persistent. He will not let us go. We wander into His presence for brief moments of divine inspiration, and then wander back out. We settle for occasional encounters with God instead of living in His presence. We are God-chasers instead of God-pleasers.

Longing for His Presence

Like countless other modern-day spiritual pilgrims who have been in pursuit of God, I had arrived at the place where I was no longer satisfied with a glimpse of His presence. It didn't matter anymore that I was a pastor and leader. I just wanted to be in His presence.

This is precisely where I found myself on the sixth day of May 1997. After thirty years of ministry, and months of spiritual dryness and perfunctory performance of my duties as the pastor of a local church, I finally paused, in desperation, to seek the Lord. I am ashamed to admit that I was so neglectful of spiritual discipline for so long, but it is the truth. Personal prayer, Bible reading, and worship were simply not a part of my daily routine, let alone my weekly or monthly schedule. God seemed far away, and I had become so busy with the ministry of the Lord that I had neglected the Lord of the ministry.

I sat alone at home on my recliner with the study door closed. I dusted off my unused journal, and it lay open on my lap. I waited in silence. My unuttered, simple plea was, "Lord, speak to me." After a few moments, I recognized that still small voice that I hadn't heard for so long. I knew it was Him!

Neglect Will Harden Your Heart

The words of the Lord resounded in my ear. "My son, just as cholesterol coats the arteries and restricts the flow of blood in your physical body, so *neglect* will harden your heart and clog your spiritual ears, restricting the flow of My Spirit and My Word to you. The enemy comes to distract you. The world calls and beckons you. There is a multitude of things that demand your attention, but above all, your flesh draws back from Me and insists on being catered to."

I heard the Father say, "You must decide! You must activate your will. Your problem is not your geographic location or your circumstances. It is you! You must return to the Secret Place with Me. As you do this on a consistent basis, I will restore you, and the flow of My Word and intimacy with Me will return.

"Come to Me! I long for communion with you. I have much for you to do. I have cleared the path and opened the heavens. Out of the Secret Place shall break forth new things. I will birth My purpose and destiny in you and through you. Come and be renewed. I love you, son. Let Me be your Father!"

It had been so long since I had heard the Lord so clearly. I went away refreshed and greatly encouraged. It was like a drink of fresh water from a pure, sparkling fountain. I was determined to return the next day to seek Him. This is what I had been missing.

A Renewed Mind

The following day when I returned to my study, I came with a burdened heart. I realized how desperately I needed to change my thought patterns. My mind was filled with worldly ideas and burdens. I had been brainwashed by the media and desensitized by prolonged exposure to the entertainment industry. My mind was polluted. Little did I realize the extent of my spiritual deterioration. My heartfelt request before Him was, "Lord, I need to have my mind renewed."

His response was instantaneous. "Son, again I say that it is a choice you must make. Have I not said, 'Whatever is pure, just, holy, and of good report, think on these things'? (See Philippians 4:8.) The enemy would seek to destroy you by using your mind as an avenue to your soul. Am

God is able to cleanse your thoughts and renew your mind.

I not able to cleanse? Am I not able to renew? Am I not able to erase? If I can cast your sins into the sea of forgetfulness, can I not also cleanse your thought life? But you must choose. Daily, you must make choices, moment by moment.

"Listen carefully. You must renew your mind in My Word. Focus your thoughts upon My will and My purposes. I have come to unbind your mind because you have asked Me to. You are not limited, as you perceive. You have placed limits upon yourself. These are not My limitations. My creativity, My anointing, and My revelation will flow through your thoughts if you will do as I say.

"You must select what will be displayed on the screen of your mind. You must choose the channel. You must decide to allow good things to occupy your thoughts and enter through the gates of your eyes and ears. My grace is sufficient for you. Fix your eyes on Me. We will overcome this stronghold of the enemy together. Then great release shall come to your life and ministry."

Yield to Me

The very next day, I began my time with the Lord by praying and interceding for my family and the flock that I pastored. I prayed specifically for an open heaven over our church. I asked the Lord to send revival and to release the spirit of evangelism. I was desperate to see growth spiritually and numerically. What I didn't realize was that God wanted to grow *me* first.

I unburdened my heart as I lifted my concerns and requests to God, and then I quieted my spirit. "What would You say to me, Lord Jesus?" I asked.

Again, He responded immediately. "I can do all the things you have asked of Me today, but you must seek My will and My kingdom first. Son, it is My pleasure to bless you, but I want you to walk in faithfulness to Me. I am preparing you to be launched into a new dimension of My work.

"Attune your ear to Me. Learn to hear My voice clearly.[1] Do not worry about self-preservation or your personal wants. Simply trust Me. I have so many wonderful things for you. My Holy Spirit is with you and in you. If you observe My instruction, My anointing will increase in the days to come.

"The past is over and finished. No more going back! Set your eyes on Me. Your success will be found not in doing what others do, but rather in yielding to My Holy Spirit. You must learn to yield to Me! This is My mandate to you. Yield to Me, and obey My voice."

Entangled Again

For three days I had been faithful to seek the Lord and spend time in His presence. I knew that He had spoken to me. But the fruit of those three days quickly dissipated as I became entangled again with the responsibilities of administering the church. My study remained empty while I tended to whatever seemed important at the moment. It was springtime, and the care of twenty acres of untended church grounds fell upon my shoulders. The sweetness of His presence quickly faded, and I found myself mowing the lawn instead of seeking Him.

Unlike Brother Lawrence, who mastered the secret of discerning the Lord's presence in the practical and often mundane activities of life, I was unable to hear His voice.[2] I knew conceptually that the Lord is present in every aspect of life, but I felt like one of the Old Testament priests who had been restricted to duty in the outer courts. It is true that cleaning the holy utensils and carrying the firewood for the altar of sacrifice were vital to the ministry of the tabernacle, but I longed for the intimacy that can be experienced only in the Holy of Holies. I was making the wrong choices, and they were leading me further and further from communion with Him. It wasn't long until I was worse off than at first.

In the middle of June, Eunice and I left Farmington, Connecticut, and traveled to New Wilmington, Pennsylvania, to spend several days with our son, Brian, his wife, Lorrie, and our two grandchildren, Aaron and Brianne. This is usually a special joy and treat for us. They live so far away, and we cherish every opportunity to share in the experiences of our grandchildren as they grow up.

This trip, however, was far from pleasant for me. I had been dissatisfied and unhappy for months, and I was miserable inside. I was frustrated, angry, resentful, negative, critical, and depressed. I was fed up with the ministry and angry with God and everyone else. It didn't take long for my son to notice my moodiness and withdrawal from the family.

No Passport

That very evening, God spoke to me in a dream.[3] The dream began with a night scene. Two of the people from our church, Tim and Kim Riley, were in a hotel with Eunice and me. The four of us were preparing to leave for a missions trip to India. We carried our baggage out to the street and were about to enter the subway that would take us to the airport. I told everyone to check to see if they had everything, when suddenly I realized that I didn't have my own passport. I knew immediately that this delay would mean that we would not make it to the airport on time if we took the subway as we had planned. I told the others to hail a cab and have it waiting when I returned. Then I dashed back into the hotel to get my passport.

Before me was a series of glass doors that were all locked, but I still had the hotel key in my possession. I opened the first one with the key and ran up the stairway to the second door. I opened it also, and then ran up the second flight of stairs to another landing. On this landing I encountered a set of glass doors. I could see that these doors led into a bank. I stood there helplessly looking through them. I knew intuitively that my key would not work on the bank doors. My only option was to wait until someone opened them from inside.

God speaks to us in many ways, including dreams and visions.

As I waited, I observed another set of stairs ascending behind me, but I knew it would be illegitimate to proceed up them. All the while, I felt a sense of panic and urgency. I was frustrated by the time that was quickly elapsing, and I was fearful that we might miss our plane.

The scene suddenly changed, and I found myself going back down to the ground level on a long escalator. When I returned to the street, there were two big limousines at the curb. Tim, Kim, and Eunice were sitting in the front limo. They were on a bench-type seat, facing out. The vehicle looked similar to one of the trams at Disney World, on which the sides open up to allow passengers to enter easily. All of our baggage had been loaded, and everyone was just waiting for me to arrive.

My concern about not having my passport was no longer an issue. It didn't seem to matter anymore. We set off for the airport, and although there was still a possibility that we could miss the plane, the chances of making it were good. The dream ended.

I Am the Problem

Early the next day, I shared the dream with Eunice as we sat on Brian's front porch in the warm country sunshine drinking our morning coffee. I told her how significant the dream was to me. "It describes my life and how I feel," I said. "I am all packed up and ready to go, but I have no passport. I feel like a man with an unfulfilled destiny who is locked inside a prison. I can't get free. I am so frustrated."

I knew that I could not blame other people or circumstances for my awful state. It was my fault. My relationship with God was almost non-existent. I was trying to fill the emptiness inside me with material things and people. I was seeking to secure my future with houses, land, and money, but it wasn't working. Even my involvement in the ministry did not satisfy me.

The longer we talked together, the more I realized that I needed to get my focus off myself. All my attention was on me! Me, me, me! I was neglecting the only thing that could help me regain my focus and balance. The thing that was missing in my life was *communion with God.*

I saw myself like a gyroscope that had lost its self-contained center of gravity because it had stopped spinning. It no longer revolved around its central point of reference. It kept wobbling and falling over. *The problem was in the center of me!* My life needed to be refocused on Jesus.

My thoughts went back to a season in my life, years before, when I had attended annual Christian Life Conferences every July. During the weeklong conference, I would spend three hours of each morning with the Lord. Those times were so fulfilling and satisfying, and I always came away from them renewed. I knew that I needed to recover that place of communion with the Lord. I felt like the Prodigal Son, who had gone away from his father. The only thing that could remedy my deplorable condition was to return to my Father's house.

Doors of Spiritual Passage

In a moment of divine inspiration, the interpretation of my dream began to unfold. The first door represented my new birth experience. When I was fifteen years old, I gave my life to Jesus Christ. I knew at that moment that He had called me into the ministry. I had stepped through a spiritual door of faith into a new and wonderful life in Christ.

The second door represented the baptism in the Holy Spirit. I received the infilling of the Spirit at Duquesne University in Pittsburgh, seven years after my spiritual birth. A devout Catholic nun prayed for me and laid hands upon me. This baptism launched me into an incredible time of spiritual growth and an awareness of a much greater spiritual dimension than I had previously experienced. The same key of faith that worked on the first door was the key that opened this second one.

But now the Lord had brought me to a new spiritual doorway, which led to intimacy and revelation regarding His purposes and destiny for my life. I would not be permitted to ascend the next set of stairs until He granted me the right to proceed. I needed a spiritual passport.

No wonder I am unhappy, I thought. *It is obvious that God will not let me go any further. I have come to a standstill. I do not have my passport, and time is running out. All the doors that I have opened with the key of faith won't get me to where the provision is, in God's bank, for this stage of my life. I have been locked out from the riches God has for me. The bank doors can be opened only from the inside,* **and that will require my waiting on God.** *I must stand on the landing* *and wait for Him to come and open the door into His presence. The key is in His hands!*

The Nature of Revelation

A long-forgotten memory flashed into my mind. As part of my early preparation for the ministry, I attended Boston University School of Theology. One of the classes that I was required to take was an overview of the New Testament. I vividly recalled one particular morning when I sat with the professor and twelve other students around a rectangular oak table in the small, modest classroom. We were discussing the nature of revelation.

I will never forget the words of the professor as he likened the revelations of God to a window or doorway in heaven. He told us that God is the only One who can initiate revelation. No matter how hard we may try to peek into the eternal things and understand His mysteries and secrets, our human efforts fail. Only He decides when to open the door or draw back the curtain and let us see into His presence. Then, He closes the curtain of revelation again. Just one momentary glimpse into His mysteries and wisdom brings enlightenment beyond any human understanding or study. My professor's words made an indelible impression upon my spirit.

Intimacy with God is the next step in your spiritual journey.

Now, years later, I realized at once that this was what the third door represented in my dream; it was the door of intimacy with God, the door of revelation and mystery. The fact that it was a double door made perfect sense to me in light of this truth. Intimacy with God would release two things—revelation *knowledge* and divine *wisdom.*

It all became clear to me. If I would wait on Him, He would move me into His presence with great care and attention. It would not occur because of my human effort. Instead, it would be by divine grace. He would replace the subway—the slower means of transportation, due to the frequent stops and starts—with a limousine, which would carry me directly and expeditiously into His presence. I was very aware that I could

47

still miss His purpose if I did not follow His instructions. But what incredible treasures awaited me in His bank of wisdom and revelation? I would know only if I obeyed Him!

Get a Life

As we drove back to Connecticut later that day, Eunice told me that the previous night, just before my dream, she had a conversation with our son, Brian. As she shared with him her concern for me, as well as her deep frustration, Brian's response was, "Dad needs to get control of his life!"

The words stung my heart! My first response was anger. But I quickly realized that Brian was absolutely right, and that God had provided the answer to my dilemma. God had given me the solution in my dream. I needed my passport in order to proceed with His purpose for my life, and I could get it only by waiting at the entrance into His dwelling place. What I needed more than anything else in life was intimacy with Him. If I waited upon Him, He would open the door.

Chapter Three

The End of
the Beginning

The surface of the church pond was frozen solid. A dusting of snow had sprinkled the ground with splotches of white like earthbound clouds on a painted landscape. Twinkling, multi-colored lights glistened in the night darkness, proclaiming the holiday season. For weeks, we had been observing Christmas. The busyness of church activities had finally slowed, and the traditional gifts and presents were already put into use or exchanged for something more suitable.

It was the last day of the year. Midnight had almost arrived, and in cities around the world people were gathering to welcome the New Year. We were about to enter the final days of the 1900s. Nineteen ninety-nine was the end of the beginning, as far as I was concerned. I had a keen sense that we were living in the days described in Matthew 24:8, which reads, *"All these are the beginning of sorrows"* (NKJV). Jesus called it *"the beginning of sorrows,"* but an alternate translation of this phrase would be "labor pains."

I was not troubled by the doomsayers or worried by all the apocalyptic warnings. My greatest concern was that we might miss the incredible opportunities that God was preparing for us in the days ahead. This was not a time for doom and gloom; it was a time to welcome the release of God's purposes in the earth. His great plan for mankind and His church, predetermined from the beginning of creation, was unfolding before our very eyes. The nations were crying out in labor pains, and the church was groaning with the fullness of God's purpose. The greatest days of spiritual harvest were still ahead.

The Longing of My Heart

Early the next morning, January 1, I made my way to my study to seek God's presence. I felt such urgency in my spirit. I desperately needed to hear from God. These were critical days, and I knew I could not go on without His presence and guidance. I trusted that He would show me everything I needed to know, for He has declared, *"I know the plans that I have for you"* (Jer. 29:11). He knows exactly what He wants to do in your life, exactly how He wants to use you.

I found myself asking again for His forgiveness and mercy as the words poured forth from my heart. "Busy, busy, busy!" I said, confessing to Him. "There are so many choices to make, Lord, and so often I choose the thing at hand rather than You. It seems like everything else takes precedence over You. Even the most mundane and insignificant things divert my attention and keep me from spending time in Your presence. I feel like the tail is wagging the dog. So much of what I am doing is administrative and mind-driven. I am like a robot going through the motions, just pretending to be spiritual, but inside I long for stillness and quiet intimacy with You. Your presence seems unattainable. You seem so distant. Even my sense of calling and anointing is at low ebb. I feel so incompetent to minister to others. My well is dry, Lord. The intensity of life has drained me spiritually.

"But You are so faithful and loving, Lord! Your grace and mercy are like precious stones of inestimable value. They shine with a brilliance that is incomparable to worldly things. I am so sorry, Lord! I have neglected the greatest thing. I have gone whoring after the world and personal pleasures. How could I be so blind, so unbelieving? Lord, restore my first love for You this year—not for the sake of what I must *do,* not so that I can be a minister and succeed, but rather because You are more than my Father and my God; You are my best friend.

"Help me to make the right choices today and in the days to come. My life with You, devotionally and intimately, has been so neglected. *Today this changes!* Make me spiritually alive again. Teach me Your ways, Lord, and grace me to be a man after Your own heart. (See Acts 13:22.) Teach me how to be a spiritual father. (See I Corinthians 4:15.) Help me to be the kind of person You desire me to be, in every aspect of my life.

God is faithful and loving, even when we are not.

"Above all, I desire to hear Your voice and to know Your will and Your ways. I want to be a good pastor and leader and a faithful servant. *Lord, let me be like Enoch.* I long to be Your friend! I want to walk with You just as Enoch did."

The Thaw

I paused to hear what the Lord might say to me. God will speak to us when we wait upon Him. Consider how many times the New Testament records Christ's words, *"He who has ears to hear, let him hear."*[1] God wants to speak to all His children, including me and you. He has much to say, if we will only listen!

As I waited on God, a keen awareness of His presence filled the room. My eyes were closed, and instantaneously I saw a vision of a frozen pond with thick, white ice covering it. People were coming to skate on the pond. The ice formed a hard, cold barrier that separated them from the water underneath. The skaters were using the outer surface of the pond and enjoying it, but were oblivious to the life that existed in the depths below.

Then the Lord spoke. "You are like this pond, My son. I have put much wealth and depth in your life, but you have not allowed others to partake of it because you have grown cold, and hardened yourself. There are many people who love you and enjoy your fellowship, but you have kept them on the surface.

"But I say to you, this is the year of thawing and breaking up the ice. I am going to soften your heart. The heat of My love for you is going to melt your icy fears and intimidation. It will dissolve the hardening that has resulted from the many years of battling and warfare that you have experienced in My church. Don't be afraid, because this tenderizing in your life will be like springtime for many who have prayed for you and longed to see you released.

"You will learn a new compassion and love for people. You will weep, and your heart will overflow with understanding. My desire is to love and encourage others through you. Do not hold back any longer. You do not need to fear men or be intimidated by anyone.

"The ice is beginning to melt. This will be a year of *becoming*, not *doing*. Your success and blessing lie in being what I have destined you to be. Just as I accept you for what I have made you to be, so others will also acknowledge you for who you are in Me. True peace, rest, and fruitfulness can be found by accepting and enjoying what I have called you to be and to do. You don't need to strive anymore. Release yourself to Me, and let go!

"I am requiring you to give away to others what I have given you. Release My love, kindness, wisdom, caring, counsel, and prophecy. Teach My Word from the depths of your spirit. My truth will flow through you as you stand to minister. This is a year of depth. I will cause you to draw up wisdom and truth from My well of revelation. It will be like a drink of fresh water for everyone I send to you. Tend to the well of your spirit daily in My presence. If you will do this, I will use you to build My house."

The words of the Lord were like a key opening the door of my heart to Him. I could actually feel myself beginning to let down the barriers I had built to protect myself. Spiritual leadership and warfare produce many casualties, and I was one of them. The wounds that I had received from other Christians were certainly not uncommon or unique. You may be in the process of building walls of protection around yourself right now. You may even be nursing wounds caused by people in the church. But God is in the business of healing and restoring His soldiers, and He won't neglect to heal and restore you, as well.

The Maze

For the first three weeks of January, God continued to minister to me through several powerful visions. In the first vision, God gave me a picture of a very large, square-shaped maze. I was suspended high above it, looking down from a sufficient height to see the entire enclosure. It was a massive labyrinth with many corridors and passageways, all seeming to lead to dead ends.

In this vision, I saw myself entering the maze. As I tried to find my way through it, it was impossible to know which way to turn. I became frustrated and hopelessly lost. I quickly realized that the only way to get through the maze was to receive direction from Someone who had a different perspective—Someone who already knew the way through the labyrinth. If I wanted to avoid turning the wrong way and hitting the walls, I needed to have supernatural guidance. I needed God's perspective and direction.

I saw a ray of light suddenly appear over my head, encompassing me. This beam of light led me directly through the maze, and I now wasted no time or effort in my travels. Finally, I reached the exit from the maze and stepped out into an unlimited open space.

The lesson was clear. The beam of light was the presence and guidance of the Holy Spirit. The only way to make it *The only way to* through the labyrinth of life was to be led by the *make it through* Spirit. Only He can provide the necessary guid- *life's maze is to* ance that we need; only He can lead us through *follow God's* the maze of everyday living. He will speak to you, *guidance.* just as He was speaking to me, and show you the way you should go. If He could lead the Israelites to the Promised Land with a pillar of cloud by day and a pillar of fire by night, He can lead us today by His voice, especially when His Spirit lives in our hearts!

The Lord began to instruct me, saying, "I am the One who sees the big picture. I see from above the situations of life. Through My Word and My Holy Spirit, I will speak to you and guide you, My son. (See Psalm 119:105; Romans 8:14.) When you hear My voice, you must be responsive to Me. Follow My voice in your heart. Do not be misled or deceived by circumstances. I can make a way where there seems to be no way. I make roads in the wilderness. I will make My path clear to you.

"You must be very sensitive to Me. I desire to activate the prophetic calling upon your life. Do not restrain or deny My anointing upon you to prophesy. Many others, besides yourself, are in the maze of life. They desire to hear My voice also. I am raising up My prophets to speak out. My prophetic word will release revelation and power. It will bring discernment, wisdom, understanding, and direction to those who receive it. In the past you have been astounded by what I have spoken through you. Now it is time to come to an even higher level of prophecy. My desire is that you move in the prophetic realm and preach with a prophetic grace.

"The unrest that you are feeling in your spirit is a preparation for change. There is a stirring and dissatisfaction within you. You cannot return to the old ways. You cannot go back! You must move into the new thing that I am doing. You did not choose Me, but I chose you! It is My doing."

His awesome presence encompassed me like a cloud. I felt like Moses standing at the burning bush. I needed no encouragement to remove my shoes; this was holy ground indeed. God was calling me to Himself, and He was going to use me. But first He had to prepare me, and that preparation involved spending time with Him, discovering His will.

No More Regrets

"Do not have regrets!" the Lord continued, with a tone of authority. "Regret and remorse are not of Me. Regret is the consequence of unresolved past issues that fester in your soul. It causes you to be frozen in the present. It saps your strength and keeps you from productivity and progress in My purpose. I am the God of mercy, forgiveness, and grace. I do not cause you to live in regret.[2]

"Now! Right now! Release your past, and let Me cast it into the sea of forgetfulness. My servant Paul understood the great need for letting go of his past when he said,

> *Brethren, I do not regard myself as having laid hold of it yet; but one thing I do: forgetting what lies behind and reaching forward to what lies ahead, I press on toward the goal for the prize of the upward call of God in Christ Jesus.* (Phil. 3:13–14)

Paul had great reason for regrets, but he learned to focus on the present and the future. Do you see how greatly I used him?

"Lessons are learned from the past, but real change comes through positive action now and in the future. If you will let go of the past, I will bring great release to you in the days to come. Why go back through the maze? There is no life in going back.

"Today, if you hear My voice, do not harden your heart. I have great and wonderful things ahead. Please hear My voice and let go of the past. I want you to walk with Me as Enoch did. You have desired a good thing. It is My heart's desire toward you. No more regrets, son! Walk hand in hand with Me, from this day forth."

His voice faded, and in the Spirit I found myself at a desert oasis. Lush palm trees surrounded me, and a spring of fresh water beckoned me to quench my thirst. Behind me, on the horizon, were huge black clouds.

These clouds are behind me now, I reasoned. *They can no longer blind me to God's purposes. I cannot go back,* I thought. *It would be foolhardy, and even dangerous, for me. I must go on with God now. I must have faith in Him.*

I made a vow in my heart to yield my present life, and my future, to Him. "I am Your servant and disciple, Lord," I uttered prayerfully. "I want to be Your friend and walk with You. I release all my regrets to you, Father. Lead me into the future. With Your help, the past will no longer paralyze me."

The turmoil and unrest in my soul dissolved with each whispered word of prayer. I felt my trust and confidence in God being renewed.

Hope for the future was springing forth within me. I knew that the past would soon be behind me as I went forward with God.

God has great plans for your life. He doesn't want you to be encumbered by the past or fearful of the future. Let go of your regrets, and focus on Him. Take your eyes off everything else but Him. He will guide you in every step you take through the maze of life. He will take you forward into the great things He has in store for you. As you trust Him, He will not fail you, and you'll experience the same hope for the future that I felt.

The Ski Jump

A few days later, as I waited in God's presence, a picture of a ski jump flashed into my mind. I saw myself racing down the steep slope and catapulting into the air. The wind whistled past my face, blowing my hair back. My goggles were pressed against my cheeks by the force of the wind. My skis were perfectly aligned, and I held my poles at my sides, steadying them with my upper arms. I soared through the air with perfect precision and balance. The speed and view were exhilarating, and my skin tingled with excitement. What a rush!

As I watched the scene, the Lord began to tell me the meaning of what I was seeing. "Son, this is a season of great release! Spiritual momentum has been gained. You have been launched into a spiritual trajectory, and My grace is upon you. My Spirit will enable you to achieve much in a short time. You will sense the ease with which things are accomplished in the coming days. My grace is upon you! There is more grace available to you than you would ever need—grace beyond sufficiency.

"My caution to you, son, is that you must keep your balance. I have given you the necessary equipment to aid you. The goggles are required so that you can see. Clear vision and direction come from Me. The time that you spend in My presence is necessary in order to prevent your goggles from fogging up.

"The ski poles are extremely vital. They represent the people I have given to support you and to hold up your arms. Just as Aaron and Hur held up Moses' arms, so I have given you people to hold up your arms. (See Exodus 17:8–13.) You will be able to lean on them and let your weight down on them. They will help you to carry the vision and burden of My purpose.

"The skis themselves represent the two essential ingredients that you must have in order to accomplish My purpose and go where I am taking you. One ski symbolizes My Word, the Holy Scriptures. The other ski is My Holy Spirit. The Word and the Spirit must work together in unison. Ride on these, and put your trust in them, for they will hold you upright and give you proper balance. By them, I will direct your path, and you will hear My voice saying, *'This is the way, walk in it'* (Isa. 30:21).

God directs us by His Word and by His Spirit.

"This is a time of positioning. Allow Me to establish the new things that I have for you. During this season, be careful to tend the flock that I have entrusted to your care. Do not neglect them. I will give you able workers to assist you in their care. Above all, do not neglect our time together. I have much to teach you and reveal to you."

The vividness and exhilaration of this vision lingered for days, penetrating deep into my mind and spirit. It was becoming increasingly evident to me that God was healing me and preparing me for an important assignment. He was using people around me and making sure everything was in place.

God is the Master Builder of our lives. He chose us before He created the foundations of the world (Eph. 1:4)! When we follow His plan for our lives, we can't go wrong. But the only way to know His plan and His will is to spend time with Him. "Do not neglect Me," He is saying to the church. In your time with Him, He will give you everything you need to accomplish His will. He will help you to keep your balance at all times, and He will surely take you into the new things He has for you when you have grown in intimacy with Him.

The Gentle Nudge of the Master

The third vision came just as spontaneously as those that preceded it. With profound clarity, God reiterated the great importance of obeying His prompting and guidance.

In the Spirit, I saw a beautifully crafted puppet suspended and held in place by invisible chords. The delicate movements of the puppeteer determined its every gesture and posture. Anyone with less skill and dexterity would have caused the puppet's movements to appear awkward and uncoordinated. It quickly became obvious to me that the person controlling this puppet was a master craftsman. With the slightest hand motions, the marionette became lifelike. It almost seemed as if the figurine was anticipating the gentle nudges of the strings, and would respond instantly, almost by reflex.

The Lord explained, "I am teaching you to be sensitive to the gentlest nudges of My Spirit. Relax, and allow Me to move the strings of direction in your life. Just as the master puppeteer sometimes repositions the puppet with a very gentle movement, so I have been nudging you in specific directions. In the days to come, there will be much stronger movements. I am beginning to give you revelation and guidance concerning the future. That is why I have called you into My presence.

"This is a year of initiating the things that have been sitting on My launching pad of destiny. This season of preparation is almost complete. I have carefully planned the days and years ahead, and in the near future I will release to My people increasing revelation regarding My strategies. Again I say, do not neglect our time together. My prophets can learn My strategy only in My presence. Be at peace in your soul."

Spiritual Surgery

The preceding weeks of communion with God made it crystal clear to me that He was requiring some very specific changes in my life. These changes were critical if I was going to fulfill His will. I was no different from every other Christian who desires to be used by God. He has to shape us before He can pour His will and purpose through us. We are the clay, and He is the Potter. He was definitely molding me, just as He does with everyone He uses. He was repairing the broken places and fitting me for His service. I was on His operating table.

Self-protection had to go. I could no longer be inaccessible and indifferent to the people whom God had put around me. My callousness and protective facade had to be broken and dissolved. He was calling me to be compassionate, caring, and vulnerable. He was demanding transparency in His people, including me!

It was time to deal with the past and put it behind me. I could no longer afford to be encumbered by the failures and the wounds that I had incurred in previous spiritual battles. Regrets had to go! I needed to be free emotionally and spiritually in order to face the purposes of God for the future.

God had made me keenly aware of my utter need to depend upon the guidance and leading of the Holy Spirit. All future progress would require clear vision and direction. I must be sensitive to the slightest prompting of His Spirit. The Holy Spirit and the Scriptures would keep me balanced as I traveled through new spiritual territory and unfamiliar spiritual surroundings in the days ahead.

God calls us to be compassionate, vulnerable, and caring—in a word, transparent.

Something was transpiring within me! God was performing spiritual surgery on me. This was far more than seeing a vision or hearing His voice. He was healing me on the inside from deep past hurts and setting me free from crippling fears.

My heart overflowed with great joy at the privilege of sitting in His presence and hearing His voice. Such life and revelation had resulted from these few weeks of intimacy with Him that I knew I could never be satisfied with anything less. He was calling me into His presence. It was an invitation that I could not resist.

God is moving His people toward something much deeper and more significant than we have ever experienced before. A great release is coming. The church is about to be launched into a whole new dimension in the Spirit, and each of us is a part of God's plans and purposes.

But first He has to work on us, giving us a transparency before Himself and the body of Christ. We can't hold back; we can't let anything stand in the way between us and Him, whether it's a past hurt or a present fear. He needs our complete surrender, our absolute willingness to open our hearts, to hear His voice, and to follow His will.

Chapter Four

The Footsteps of Enoch

My desire to spend time in the Lord's presence increased with each passing day. The more I knew about God, the more I wanted to know. My greatest desire was to live in His presence, and each day I would eagerly retreat into my study and close out the world. God has a way of giving us the part of Himself that makes us long for more. He'll draw us into His presence and reveal Himself until we see that nothing else on this earth compares to being with Him. We won't want to live a moment without knowing He is right beside us.

In my passion for God's presence, I would enter my study, shut all the doors leading to the back of our house, disconnect the phone, and instruct my wife not to disturb me unless there is an emergency. She realized that I was determined to take my daily walk with the Lord.

On this particular morning, I again entered my study to spend time with the Lord. The lounge chair I had inherited from my father was now covered with a white bedspread in order to hide its unsightly appearance. Many years ago, the orange upholstery had frayed and worn through, exposing the foam seat cushion. To most people, the chair was fit only for the dump, but to me it was a holy place. It was my prayer chair! This is where I came to meet with the Lord.

Once I was comfortably seated, my view of our backyard through the study window helped me to calm my thoughts and enter into the Lord's presence. Our sequestered driveway is located to the left, just outside the window. It leads onto a tree-lined cul-de-sac where there is very little traffic. A pear tree stands directly outside the window, and wild blackberry bushes line the distant perimeter of the grassy backyard. A stand of stately, tall evergreens just beyond the berry bushes provides a safe haven for wild turkeys, deer, and foxes. Squirrels and chipmunks play freely in the yard, and several species of birds fly about, satisfying their hunger on the abundant fruits and berries. When I am engulfed in this solitude, it takes only a few moments to quiet my spirit and concentrate my focus on the Lord.

My journal lay open on my lap to the page where I had made my last entry. Oftentimes, I would begin my talk with the Lord by saying, "Lord, I am here. I have come to walk with You today, just as Enoch did so many years ago." These very words issued from deep within my heart on this early spring morning.

Adam Is My Great...Grandpa

I found myself identifying more and more with Enoch. I was so intrigued by this ancient patriarch, known to many as a friend of God. *Who was this man?* I pondered. *What was it like for Enoch, when he walked with God?* I hungered for the same intimacy and friendship with God that he must have had. I longed to be like him. I wanted to walk in Enoch's footsteps. I lifted my Bible from the end table next to my chair to find some answers to my questions. What I discovered quickly revealed why I had such an affinity for this ancient man of faith.

Enoch's father was a man by the name of Jared, a direct descendant of Seth. Enoch was part of the seventh generation removed from Adam. He was actually born six-hundred twenty-two years after Adam was created. What astounded me the most was the amazing discovery that

Adam was still alive when Enoch was born. Enoch was a contemporary with his ancient relative, Adam, for three-hundred and five years!

Can you imagine little Enoch sitting on his great grandfather's knees as a child? I am sure that great grandpa Adam told his grandson all about his own intimate walks with God in the Garden of Eden. Could it be that Enoch's desire for intimacy and fellowship with God was kindled as he heard his great grandfather speak of the wonderful things he had learned himself when he walked with God? I suspect that, with Adam's encouragement, Enoch began to take daily walks with God at a very young age.

In ancient times, the giving of a name always signified the personality and destiny of the recipient. It is no surprise that Enoch's name means "to instruct, or to initiate." It also means "dedicated, consecrated, and experienced." This name was certainly appropriate for Enoch. He *dedicated* and *consecrated* himself to walk with God. He fixed his life-purpose on intimacy and friendship with the Almighty. While Abraham walked *before* God, Enoch walked *with*

Abraham walked before God, but Enoch walked with God.

God. In that intimacy, God initiated him into the spiritual realm and *instructed* him in matters of eternal significance. Enoch became known as "the experienced one."

During his short time on earth, at least in comparison with his contemporaries, Enoch fathered many sons and daughters, including Methuselah. (Methuselah, the oldest man who ever lived, died at the ripe old age of nine-hundred sixty-nine.) Enoch was a patriarch, a man of faith (Heb. 11:5), and an anointed prophet who foretold the second coming of Christ. Many of his prophesies, visions, and dreams were written down in the three volumes of The Books of Enoch, which are part of the pseudepigrapha (a collection of Jewish religious writings from the years 200 B.C. to A.D. 200).[1] The writings of Enoch were quite popular in early Judaism, and were respected by many of the Christians in antiquity. Jude even quoted Enoch in the New Testament (Jude 14–15). The book of First Enoch is considered by some historians to be a primary source in the formation of Jewish doctrine in the last two centuries preceding the birth of Christ.

Enoch's writings are apocalyptic in nature (from the Greek *apokalupsis,* meaning "revelation" or "disclosure"). He spoke about such subjects as the angels, whom he referred to as the Watchers, identifying them by name and rank. He recounted the fall of certain evil angels, and their intermarriage with the daughters of men. He revealed the secrets of the cosmos, and the coming judgment of the wicked. His book reads like a spiritual travelogue, as he recounted his many journeys while being accompanied by God and angels. There is even an ancient legend circulated among the Arabs that Enoch was the father of writing, and that he received divine revelation.

The God-Pleasers

"Enoch walked with God; then he was no more, because God took him away" (Gen. 5:24 NIV). Enoch started out walking with God one day and never came back home. God took him, sixty-nine years before the birth of Noah, at the age of three-hundred sixty-five. Enoch saw the mysteries of the universe, the future of the world, and the predetermined course of human history. Long before the Flood, the patriarchs, and the great prophets and kings of Israel, Enoch walked with God. In that communion, he plumbed the depths of God's mysteries and secrets.

> *By faith Enoch was taken from this life, so that he did not experience death; he could not be found, because God had taken him away. For before he was taken, he was commended as one who pleased God.* (Heb. 11:5 NIV)

What greater legacy could Enoch leave than to be regarded as a God-pleaser?

Now I understood why the Spirit had drawn me to this man. He epitomized my deepest desires. I wanted, more than anything, to be pleasing to God. I valued intimacy with Him over everything else in life. I longed to know the mysteries and secrets that could only be learned by walking in His presence. I knew that there are secrets hidden in the heart of God, and that wise men draw them out. (See Proverbs 20:5.) I wanted to be a God-pleaser, just like Enoch. I, too, wanted to consecrate my life, so that the Almighty might instruct me.

This can be the life of every believer. Every one of us can come to a place where we please God and know Him intimately. His presence can abide with us constantly, guiding us in everything. Like Enoch, we can walk with God in such a personal, intimate way that the secrets of God's heart become part of our own hearts. In fact, God wants us to walk with Him as Enoch did. He longs for that kind of fellowship with each of us. The key is opening your heart to taste of God's presence. Then you'll only be hungry for more!

Only a few moments had passed since I had uttered my request to the Lord. Thoughts of Enoch filled my mind and heart, when I heard the Lord respond to my plea with a wonderful invitation. "Son, what you ask of Me is the desire of My heart also. I want our time together to be just like My time with My friend Enoch. You and I will take daily Enoch walks together."

And so, my "Enoch walks" with the Lord began in earnest. The things that He revealed to me during our first walks together were in preparation for the deeper revelations that were to follow. They were given as foundation truths, upon which to build further revelation. God always gives us exactly what we can digest. He starts us off with the basics and builds upon them. He wants to reveal Himself to you, if you will only walk with Him.

The first lesson dealt with the meaning of life. I listened carefully with an open heart as the Lord spoke.

Lesson One: The Essence of Life

"Have I not given you life to enjoy? All around you, son, are people who do not know how to live. I sent My Son Jesus to show people how to live, to enjoy a sunset, to touch the skin of a newborn baby, to take in the fragrance of a day, to live life to the fullest. Life is a gift from Me! I have made life and all things for you to enjoy.

"There are so many people who walk through life, but never live it. I am life! I am more than just ordinary life. I am the essence of life itself.

(See John 5:21, 24–26, 39–40.) I want you to be truly alive with My kind of life. (See John 1:4, 11–13.) I have given you life. I was there when you breathed your first breath. (See Psalm 139:13–16.) That is why it grieves Me when you do not live life to its fullest potential. When your senses are dulled, or you are encumbered by cares and worries so that you cannot live as I intended, My heart is saddened.

"I want you to understand that I am the Life-giver. My desire is to release My life force in all creation, especially in all mankind. When I

You can be truly alive with God's kind of life.

walked the earth in the beginning, My life force existed in the Garden. The Tree of Life was available to My creation. Adam and Eve were equally endued with life. After Adam's disobedience, sin eventually took its toll. The life force gradually dissipated, and the life span decreased. Just as the enemy came to deceive Adam and Eve and take life from them, he also comes to steal life from you. He is your enemy and adversary.

"The real issue is life or death! Many people have missed the point. So many are alive, yet dead. (See Ephesians 2:1–10.) They are dead because even while they breathe, walk, and think, they have not allowed My abundant life force to flow into them. (See 2 Corinthians 5:14–17.) Enoch understood this principle well. He was the father of Methuselah. It was My life force flowing through him that gave Methuselah longevity. Enoch knew that real life existed in Me, and that in Me there was no death. His intimacy with Me gave him life!

"Do you understand what I am saying to you? I am *life itself.* I am the life force.[2] No one lives without Me. All living things exist in Me and through Me. (See Acts 17:28.) My desire is that you allow My life force to flow into you, and through you to others. I long for people to be truly alive. Satan has come to steal, kill, and destroy life. I have come so that you might have life, abundant life. (See John 10:10.) I am revealing these things to you because you have chosen to walk with Me just as Enoch did. I am so pleased and delighted that you desire to know My truth."

The reality of this revelation seemed to penetrate the very cells of my body. *Life, divine life, supernatural life, eternal life, is so much more* than a theological concept, I thought. *It is real! It is tangible! It is Jesus! And I am experiencing it right now. Why would anyone not desire this Life?* I wondered.

Here it was, practically spelled out for me: God is the essence of life; He is Life itself. We have abundant life through Him, and we have no life without Him. To be truly alive, we must look to Him!

Lesson Two: Being, Not Doing

The very next day, as we walked together, the Lord began to instruct me regarding life's purpose.

"Today I want to speak to you about the purpose of life," He said. "Many believe that they must discover their purpose for living, that life is *about* purpose. But, in truth, life *is* purpose. Meaning is found in the fact of life itself. So many people try to find fulfillment in what they do, instead of who they are and who I am.

"Adam was formed so that I could walk with him, not so that he could tend the Garden. I did not create Adam because I needed a gardener. Work is a result of life, not the purpose and meaning of life. Your forefathers were correct when they said, 'The chief end of man is to glorify God and to enjoy Him forever.'[3]

"I have made all mankind because I desire companionship. You were made to have communion with Me; *that is your purpose and the purpose of every man and woman on earth.* Enoch discovered that his life was satisfying as long as he enjoyed communion with Me. I want you to understand this same simple truth: your fulfillment flows out of communion with Me. All things find their true meaning for existence in Me. When you separate yourself from Me, the purpose for which I created you is denied.

"When you fulfill your purpose by spending time with Me, everything that you need in order to accomplish your assignment in life is released. Fellowship with Me was Adam's purpose; tending the Garden was his assignment. Out of communion with Me comes creativity. Creativity is My life force, giving release to new potential and new things.[4] All that is needed for life, I have provided.

"Your enemy, Satan, took his focus off Me and, as a result, glorified his own ability. He thought that his reason for existence was to make music. He failed to see that his true purpose was to serve Me. He was created for My pleasure.

"Do you understand, son? Today's lesson is on being. I made you to be with Me, to enjoy Me, and to walk with Me. Everything flows out of intimacy with Me. Purpose, meaning, goals, even creativity—all these things are a result of your relationship with Me, and are enhanced by the time you spend with Me. My nature is 'I AM,' not 'I DO.' Without Me, you can do nothing. You are a human *being*, not a human *doing*. You must learn how to *be*.

"I have made you for My pleasure. I am teaching you to appreciate life and how to be fully alive. Many people are dormant and asleep, much like trees in the winter, but My life is like springtime. I am bringing you into springtime."

The words of the Lord faded into silence. Outside my study window, all the vibrant signs of spring heralded life and fulfillment. Creation itself seemed to trumpet God's purpose. But even more significantly, something was transpiring within me. I was emerging from a spiritual winter. New life was coursing through my heart. Finally, the seasons were changing for me. I was beginning to understand God's real purpose for my life. It wasn't ministry or work; it was intimacy with God! I was made in His image, for His glory and pleasure.

You were made for God's pleasure.

Do you see now why God created you? He created you to have fellowship with Him. When you spend time with Him, you are both discovering and fulfilling your purpose.

Lesson Three: The Seasons of Life

A few days later, still basking in the joy of the fresh, revitalizing presence of the Lord in my life, I approached Him with a hunger to know more about His incredible design for life. I was so intrigued by the fact that there are "spiritual seasons."

"Teach me more about the seasons, Father," I prayed. (See Ecclesiastes 3:1; Acts 1:7.)

"Seasons are different degrees or stages of life," He responded. "My life force remains intact, but it may be dormant within an individual. This is true even in nature; during the winter months the life force is resident, just waiting to be awakened. My life force exists and remains in the seed until it is released.

"The same is true of people. Though they appear dead, My spiritual life force is within them, waiting to be quickened by My Holy Spirit. Paul said,

But if the Spirit of Him who raised Jesus from the dead dwells in you, He who raised Christ Jesus from the dead will also give life to your mortal bodies through His Spirit who indwells you.

(Rom. 8:11)

"This is what happens when a person is born again. I have given natural life to all men, and within them is the capacity to believe in Me. When they come to Me in faith, My Holy Spirit releases My life force within their spirits.

"Why does life have to go through these seasons?" I questioned.

"It is the process of procreation," He replied. "Death is not cessation of life. (See Hebrews 9:27.) Instead, it is the release of life to a different dimension, an eternal dimension. Before death came, the life force was available in the Garden. The Tree of Life flourished, providing replenishment of the life force as Adam and Eve ate from it. This tree is so potent that it is able to provide for the healing of every nation. (See Revelation 22:1–2.)

"Death is part of the curse. Because of their sin, Adam and Eve were denied access to the Tree of Life. They died as a consequence. Their lives were no longer sustained by partaking of the fruit of intimacy with Me. But I have reversed the curse by raising My Son Jesus from the dead. I have reopened the way to intimacy with Me. The fruit of the Tree of Life is available again through My Son. Through Jesus, I have restored eternal life to mankind. Only by partaking of Him can you live. (See John 6:53–58.)

"A few individuals were exceptions to the curse of sin and death. Enoch did not experience death. Neither did Elijah. They were forerunners and prophetic examples of the result of intimacy with Me. They partook of the eternal Tree of Life. Their communion with Me released My life force, and they did not die. Life is released in My presence. I am the God of the living and not the dead!"

Lesson Four: Total Commitment

Intrigued by God's mention of Enoch and Elijah, I raised the question of God's reason for choosing certain individuals for His service.

"Lord Jesus," I said, "Enoch chose to walk with You, and Elijah was taken into Your presence in a chariot of fire. Even King David, despite his awful sins, was a man after Your own heart. But what about Paul? He doesn't seem to fit the same description. You chose Paul despite his utter rebellion and contempt for Your people. Was there something in this man that moved You to action?"

His response was enlightening. "Paul was a man of acute intellect and integrity, whose emotions needed to catch up with his understanding. I put him in touch with himself. When I appeared to him on the road to Damascus, his life truly began. (See Acts 9:1–22.) The issues that created the dichotomy within him were resolved. He was released into total freedom and abandonment to Me. His faith moved from his mind to his heart.

"In all the men you have mentioned, there is a common trait: total commitment to their life's purpose. Enoch's joy was to meet with Me and to commune with Me. Elijah learned to hear the whisper of My voice. David worshipped with total abandonment before the ark of My presence. Paul fixed his vision and gaze solely upon Me, and abandoned his past life. (See Philippians 3:13–14.) They were totally involved in their mission; all of them walked

Joy comes through total abandonment to God.

70

in intimacy with Me. They were men who had singleness of heart and mind. There was no duplicity or double-mindedness within them.

"I hate mixture and double-mindedness. (See Leviticus 19:19.) Very little progress is made in life when you are tossed between two opinions, two purposes, or two choices. Indecision is a crippling condition, and halfheartedness quickly weakens the resolve of those around you."

His words pierced the core of my being. *Singleness of heart,* I thought. *That is the secret! That is what God looks for in each of us.*

"Lord, I want to be a man whose heart is after You," I prayed silently. "Please let my life be filled with a burning passion for intimacy with You, Jesus."

Lesson Five: A Lavish God

His response was not what I expected.

"I am a God who lavishes blessings on My children. I love to give beyond measure, and I want you to be just like Me, especially when you worship. Be unrestrained in your worship! Be known as a lover of God! I encourage you to lavish love and praise upon Me. If you will do this, you will quickly discover that your own life will increase in abundance. If you will freely worship Me, especially when you are in the presence of others, you will be set free from the subtle pride that quickly quenches My Spirit. I want you to be an encouragement to others. Be free to worship Me without restraint, just as David did.

"I want you to be a man whose words and actions are heartfelt. You must worship and minister out of your heart, not your head. Speak and act out of the abundance of your heart where I dwell. Then when you speak, your words will express the true faith that is in your heart. (See Matthew 12:34.) Let your heart be the wellspring of godly thoughts. When you do this, your words will carry a powerful anointing and set others free to worship and believe in Me."

"Lord," I replied, "You know the secrets of my heart. You know every hidden thing. Surely You know that I love you."

The First Law of the Spirit

His words were reassuring but firm. "I do know that you love Me. But do not be ashamed to let others know that you love Me.

"I am much more than wisdom and knowledge. I am *Love!* Enoch, Elijah, David, and Paul all came to understand that I am love. You cannot walk with Me and not be impacted and changed by My love for you. You will be, and you are being, changed by My love. Receive My love. Bask in My love. Come, walk with Me in My love!

"I am the center of everything. Do you remember the gyroscope I showed you months ago?[5] I was seeking to reveal to you that in Me all things consist and have their being. (See Acts 17:28; Romans 11:36.) This is the first law of the Spirit. I am the force of life that holds the worlds, the universe, and the smallest particles yet to be discovered, in place. My glory indeed covers the earth. If you discern correctly, you will see My presence everywhere. Without Me, nothing was made that was made. (See John 1:3.) I am love, but I am also energy. When I manifest My glory, energy is released; pure light, creative power, and life force radiate from My being. I am the Giver of life. I am the Light of the world."

The Inner Court

What had previously been only head knowledge began to filter into my heart as the Lord spoke to me. God was no longer unapproachable or unknowable. This is what happens when we spend time with Him. He will manifest Himself to our hearts, and we will know Him intimately. He will be the center of our lives, and all life will radiate from Him. We will be able to approach Him without hesitation, with the full understanding that we can know Him.

God was performing a transformation in my life. I was moving from the outer court to the inner court, nearer to His presence. He was actually becoming my life source.

I was impacted by the truth that Adam and Eve did not die because of sin. It was true that their sin precipitated God's response of judgment, but their actual death was a result of no longer eating the fruit of the Tree of Life. Access to the Tree of Life was restored through Jesus Christ. He is life! No man can come to the Father except through Him. (See John 14:6.) Life really flows out of intimacy with God, and that intimacy is available only through the way that Jesus has prepared for us. If you want to truly *live,* then spend time with God each day.

Unlike Adam, who was denied access to the life force, I was eating of the Tree of Life; I was discovering the reality of intimacy with Jesus. Like Enoch, I was walking daily in His presence. This was not theory; this was experiential. Through intimate communion, God was moving me toward total commitment and singleness of heart. I really wanted to lavish my love and worship upon Him with total abandonment, and it didn't matter anymore what others might think about me. I knew there could be no mixture. If I was going to walk with Him, I must turn away from the world's allure and distractions.

I was finally regaining my spiritual equilibrium. My center of focus was restored. Just as God had placed the Tree of Life in the center of the Garden of Eden, He was adjusting my life so that I would be centered on Him. One singular thing made every other activity and responsibility meaningful in my life. *Everything pales in comparison with intimacy with God.* It was my daily "Enoch walk" with the Lord. I began to understand why Enoch decided not to return from His walk with God one day. Everything else seemed to pale in comparison with intimacy with God.

I knew that this was God's desire, not only for me, but also for every person He has brought into this world. The fruit of the Tree of Life is available to everyone! You and I can walk in Enoch's footsteps because of Jesus. He has prepared the way by His death on the cross for our sins. Intimacy and communion with God in the Spirit is life-giving and life-sustaining; it will not only give you life as it was truly meant to be, but it will also *keep* you in that abundant life.

Chapter Five

A Holy Spirit Explosion

The sound washed over me like water cascading down a cliff, leaping from rock to rock, pounding and crashing its way into the pool of my spirit. I was standing next to the three-foot-high platform as the musicians worshipped the Lord.

I had never seen such an eclectic set of drums and percussion instruments like this in all my life. There were acoustic and electronic drums combined. A maze of chrome scaffolding held chimes, bells, gourds, and plates, not to mention some items that I had never seen before. An array of cymbals whispered with subtle innuendo, and then crashed with forceful declaration.

A New Sound

Enclosed on three sides by this scaffolding of instruments, the drummer moved with an ease and grace that revealed his skill and experience. But far more impressive than this was a powerful anointing that emanated from this blending of percussion, musical instruments, and voices as the group ministered to the Lord.

Never had I heard such a sound! It was the expression of a new generation of believers. It rose up into the heavenlies and cried out for God to come and visit His people. It was pure, unabashed praise, and yet at times it was also intimate, tender worship.

For three hours, I stood transfixed as this music penetrated my soul and spirit. Deep called to deep as the aboriginal didgeridoo sounded its reverberating bass tones, and the synthesizer echoed an ethereal sound of heavenly strings. I was totally engulfed by the music. I was caught up into an atmosphere of revelation. Something was happening to me, and God was in it.

It was a Wednesday night, and we had joined hundreds of other *A new sound of explosive worship is arising from this generation.* believers to experience this unique expression of praise and worship. We were crowded into a darkened country dance hall that had recently been converted into a church. This worldly edifice now served as a gathering place for worship and other Christian events. The distinct nonreligious feel permeating the room was so wonderfully refreshing. Despite the location, the power and presence of God was electrifying.

I left the concert that evening near midnight, after visiting the tape and CD table and purchasing everything available. I had to have this music! There was something about it that activated my spirit and drew me into God's presence. I added these newly obtained CDs to the stack that I had purchased in Charlotte just a few days earlier.

The following Saturday, my wife and I left Charlotte early in the morning. After a short visit with our son, Scott, his wife, Andrea, and our three grandchildren, Brandon, Joanna, and Anthony, in Winston Salem, we resumed our journey home to Connecticut. Little did we realize that God had started His clock ticking, and we were caught up in a divine plan that would culminate, the following day, in a powerful supernatural encounter in the Spirit. The next few hours would be a time of preparation for what God had planned for the next morning.

We marked the passing miles, not by the highway signs, but by the CDs placed in the player. Each new song carried a powerful anointing. At one point, the presence of God so filled the car that my wife and I were unable to speak. Tears streamed down our faces and fell on our laps. The weight of His glory pressed us into the seats, and we felt as though we would burn up with the heat of His presence. For twelve hours, worship and sweet, intimate fellowship with the Lord Jesus Christ inundated us. I fell into bed that night with the music still reverberating in my soul and spirit.

Holy Fire

That same Saturday, hundreds of miles to the north, Donna Gollenberg, one of the worship leaders at The Potter's House, was preparing for the following morning's worship service. She was alone in the living room of her home, listening to a CD entitled *Holy Fire*. As she began to walk around the room singing along with each song on the CD, she sensed the Holy Spirit prompting her to go and get her flute. Placing the beautifully crafted, silver instrument to her lips, she started to accompany the music. Pure worship filled the room.

For ten minutes she played; the notes tumbled forth with delicate precision and tender expression. It was a musical prayer. It became the cry of her heart to the Lord. Suddenly, God's holy presence filled the room. His power and glory overwhelmed her. She fell to her knees in humility before Him. In that place of utter surrender, all she could do was cry out, "O God, consume me, consume me! Let me be a holy sacrifice to You. Consume me with Your holy fire." In that moment, she wanted nothing else but Him. She was so totally surrendered that she whispered, "Lord, if You want to take me home right now to be with You, I am ready to go."

These events were happening simultaneously. In the very same moments that the Lord was visiting her in her home, He was also visiting us in our car. It was no coincidence. A crescendo of worship and praise was beginning to build, and we were all caught in the powerful flow of the Holy Spirit. What we didn't realize was that we were headed for a spiritual Niagara Falls.

An Angel Doorman

Early Sunday morning, Donna Roy, one of the intercessors at our church, felt prompted to take a morning walk. Her normal routine is to walk only on weekdays. Sunday is usually busy enough, with getting the family ready and out the door in time for Sunday worship, but this day was different. She had a divine appointment.

As she walked, the Lord gave her a vision. She saw a very tall angel standing at the entry door to our church. This angel was so tall that she could see up to only his shoulders. The angel would not permit anyone to pass by him to enter the church without discarding his or her baggage and leaving it at the door. There were suitcases and backpacks of all colors stacked in piles just outside the church entrance. Some people tried to sneak by the angel undetected, but he would grab them by their shirts or blouses. He even made some of them empty their pockets. No one was allowed to enter without leaving his or her burdens and cares outside the door.

Tapped into God

I arrived at the church that morning a few minutes late for worship rehearsal. The other singers and musicians had already gathered for prayer and were standing on the platform in a circle with their hands joined. There was an unusual sense of God's presence. I removed my saxophone from its case and approached the others on the platform. Immediately, I sensed the Lord leading me to lay hands on our chief musician, Quigley Foran, and pray for him. As I did so, without wanting to interrupt what the others where praying for, he fell to his knees and began to worship the Lord.

At this point, Donna Gollenberg (the appointed worship leader for that morning, who had already encountered the living God in her home the day before) began to weep uncontrollably. The entire worship team seemed to be tapped into God.

I moved to our keyboard player and took her hands in mine. I began to pray, "Lord, these hands are hands of fire. These are fingers of fire,

Lord. Let Your holy fire anoint these hands as they play for You today. Let Your anointing flow through these hands to release Your presence in this place. Let them be hands of fire, Lord!"

No Ordinary Prayer Meeting

The intercessors usually gather in my office thirty minutes before each Sunday service to pray together, and to receive their prayer assignments for that morning's meeting, but today was to be no ordinary prayer time. As they began to intercede, the presence of the Lord filled the room. Donna Roy was lying on the floor of the office, laughing hilariously. Next to her, Jean Redekas, the wife of one of our deacons, was also lying on the floor, crying and sobbing uncontrollably. On the other side of my desk, her

Time spent in God's presence is never ordinary.

husband, Gary, a tall man of about six feet four inches, was stretched out on the carpet almost wall to wall, praying fervently for the meeting that was about to begin upstairs. It took them several minutes to gain enough composure to make their way upstairs.

An Explosion of the Holy Spirit

The members of the worship team took their places to begin the meeting. Donna was standing at the pulpit as the first notes of the opening worship song began to sound forth. We had only sung the first few lines of the lyrics when something supernatural happened. We were instantly caught up into the heavenlies. Donna crumpled to the floor in front of the pulpit, unable to move. No one was leading worship any longer. The Holy Spirit had taken over.

The entire worship team was launched into a level of musical ability that far exceeded their natural talents. Sounds were being played, and notes were issuing forth, that went far beyond anything we had ever experienced. The chief musician had his eyes closed. He was lost in the Lord as he played his guitar. The drummer, who was the newest member of the team, and just a beginner, sounded like he had been playing for years.

As the worship continued, my eyes scanned the congregation in amazement. People were weeping and crying, and some were kneeling or lying prostrate on the floor. The youth were sitting in the aisles with tears streaming down their faces as others prayed for them. The children were waving flags and streamers before the Lord. The most amazing thing was that everyone was involved. No one was merely observing. There was total participation, and it was all being orchestrated solely by the Holy Spirit.

At one point in the progression of worship, I sensed that we needed to move into a warfare mode. I tried to get the attention of our chief musician, but he still had his eyes closed. I moved into the orchestra section and said to the guitar player, "We need to do a warfare song." He nodded his head in agreement. The Lord had already spoken to him. Unbeknownst to me, one of the men from the congregation had just begun to give a powerful prophecy regarding the kingdom of God and the Lord's intentions in the earth.

The tempo changed with precision timing, and a marchlike rhythm sounded from the musicians. The congregation marched around the circumference of the auditorium, warring in the heavenlies. I could hear the worship flags snapping along with the cadence of the music.

Two hours had passed, but it seemed like only a few minutes. Time stood still, as we worshipped under the direction of the Holy Spirit. Then the unusual anointing lifted slightly. I approached the podium to receive the morning offering. I paused for a moment, in silence. Finally, I said to the congregation, "Well, I think the Lord has accomplished His purpose for today. I am not going to preach. Let's just go home."

The entire congregation erupted in spontaneous applause. They knew instinctively that nothing else was needed. The deepest longings of their hearts had been fulfilled. The Lord had come into our midst, and His awesome glory and love had washed over us. We had been caught up into the supernatural realm of His presence.

Supernatural Results

Worship had begun at 10:00 A.M., and it was now almost 1:00 in the afternoon. For the next two hours, people lingered in the auditorium, still basking in the presence of the Lord. It seemed that no one wanted to leave. One of the teenagers, who was visibly moved by the meeting, came to me and said, "Pastor, I saw what looked like a bolt of lightning come out of the wall speaker and strike the floor at the front of the platform."

For the next few days, we received phone calls and personal reports of the supernatural things that had occurred. One woman was taken back in time and experienced a powerful healing. Children and adults saw visions. Angels appeared to some individuals. In fact, at one point after the meeting was dismissed, I was walking near the front of the auditorium and sensed the presence of an angel. The only person I saw was a man named Michael, who happened to be lying on the floor, slain in the Spirit, near where I was standing; so I asked the angel, "Who are you?"

The angel replied, "I cannot tell you, for I have been sent to Michael."

I leaned over to Michael and said, "Michael, there is an angel here, and he claims that he was sent to you."

Without a moment's hesitation, Michael responded, "I know! I have just met him."

Several days later, one of the mothers reported to me the following story. She was getting her two-year-old daughter, Jenna, ready for bed that evening and said to her, "Let's say our bedtime prayers." Her daughter immediately began to shout loudly in tongues. She had never prayed in the Spirit before. The Lord had sovereignly filled her with the Holy Spirit and given her a language of prayer during the worship service!

The spiritual realm is more real than the physical one.

For months, I had been sensing that God was getting ready to do something awesome in our congregation. There was a building anticipation and expectancy among us. I had told the congregation that we were headed for a Holy Spirit explosion. I thought that it would happen when some guest speaker or visiting ministry was with us. God had different plans! He just took over and moved us into a spiritual dimension of intimacy and revelation that suddenly made the spiritual world more real than the physical one.

A Door Is Opened

The very next morning, I rushed to my study to seek the Lord. "Lord, what's happening?" I asked. "What are You doing?" I desperately needed some answers. I knew that what had happened had a much greater significance and purpose than what was obvious to me at first. God wanted to do more than just visit us. I sensed that He was initiating something strategic.

"I have opened a door in the heavenlies," He responded. (See Psalm 78:23–25.) "There is no latch on it, but it swings back and forth. It is the door of My presence. I have broken the seal and released the lock. I bid you now to come in and out of the Holy Place. This will be a house of priestly worship. Angels will come to assist you, for I have called you to release the heavenly sound.

"As Moses struck the rock and life-giving water poured forth, so yesterday in worship you struck the rock of My presence. The river has been released. Deep calls unto deep. There has been an impartation. I have called you to release the heavenly music. Your hands are anointed to make war on behalf of the saints. It is time to march into My purposes.

"I will give you My strategies, for I am sending forth from this place, and from many other places, an army of worshippers who are My Holy Spirit-anointed priests. I have summoned them to go before the army of My saints to praise Me.

"Strategy flows out of intimacy with Me. Continually wash yourself with My anointed music and praise. It will be, as you come in and out through the door of My presence, that angels will accompany you.

Cherubim and seraphim will know you by name. My key of anointed music will unlock the secrets of the heavenlies.

"Press forward now with My strategic plans. Do what I instruct you to do. These are critical matters. Therefore, I extend My abundant grace to you. I give you a full and complete grace to do My will. Be released in My grace, and I will release great joy and fruit as a result.

"Do not try to imitate or duplicate what others are doing. Just let My Spirit flow. Release others around you, for I have sent them. I am preparing a construction team, like a bulldozer, to clear great stretches of land and forest for Me, in order to complete my end-time purposes.

"Delight in Me! Delight in Me, son, for I delight in you. I have rejoiced with My angels and have released My joy in the heavenlies. You will see My angels. I will open your eyes to see the heavenly messengers, for they are all around you and stand as a wall of fire completely encircling those I have called into end-time ministry. They encompass My worshippers.

"Signs and wonders, yes, signs and wonders will begin to occur throughout the church. Get ready! Do not worry or concern yourself with crowds or with growth. Just obey Me. I demand holiness and purity. Let holiness and purity proceed from My throne room. My purifying fire is being released upon the earth. I am cleansing My church of impurity. No more pollution! I call you to turn away from those things that will pollute you and My house. Do not pollute My holy stream by exposure to worldly pleasures or media."

God was speaking to me with a message for the church. I knew that He wanted me to proclaim all that He was telling me. His call to holiness was not just for me, but for the entire body of Christ. God's purifying fire is coming upon all believers, but the rewards of obedience are great. Begin to delight in the Lord, and He will give you the joy He has promised.

A Psalm of Worship

A heavenly sound began to play through my spirit as I sat in God's presence. Words began to pour forth spontaneously out of my heart.

They flowed unto the Lord, like the words of the shepherd, warrior, and king, David. It was a psalm of worship.

> The sound, the sound, the sound, O God!
> The sound of the mountains,
> The crashing of the oceans,
> The wind.

> "I play the mountains," says the Lord.
> "The whole earth is a symphony, an instrument of praise.
> The wind in the forest,
> The birds and animals,
> The whistling canyons,
> The crash of thunder,
> The bolt of lightning, a conductor's rod.
> The sounds of creation, the creative sounds!
> The beginning of sound.
> Listen to the sounds of worship.
> The stars as twinkling chimes,
> The explosion of the timpani of the thunderous waves,
> The still sound of the growing fields,
> The strings of the wheat field,
> And the castanets of the crickets.
> The bongo frogs, and the rattling maracas of the humble rattle-snake.

> "The whole earth is an instrument of praise and worship.
> A continual chorus of worship to the Creator.

> "The brook, the waterfall, the river, the stream.
> It flows with endless strength.
> It sings to Me.
> It crashes as a mighty waterfall, cascading over the edge.
> It skips with a melody of joy and lighthearted freedom.
> It moves as a deep-flowing river with great strength and confidence.

No man can dam it up or stop its flow.
Where they have tried,
I simply overflow the banks and cut a new channel in which to
flow.

"My river is flowing, flowing, flowing.
Move with My current.
Let Me take you on.
Let Me take you on."

Then I heard the Lord say, "I am awakening the earth anew to release My sound. It is the sound that pleases Me. This sound is beginning to rise and ascend from the earth. The mountains and the hills sound forth My praises. This sound is going forth into the universe. It is the declaration of the King. The earth is the transmitter of a heavenly sound.

"In the earth, I am awakening My bride. I am calling you, My bride, to break forth into singing. I have released the heavenly choir. As the angels sang at My birth, now they have joined the human sound, to accompany your praise. There is a sound going forth. It has begun! It has begun!"

No More Religion

The tone of His voice suddenly grew stern and commanding. "This is a day of release! All religion must be swept away. Man has tried to stop the flow of My Spirit. NO MORE! I HAVE HAD ENOUGH!" The Lord spoke with fear-inspiring resolve. "Religion has sought to kill My Spirit and stop the flow.[1] NO MORE!

"Religion must be cut away. I will no longer tolerate it in My house. Just as I overturned the tables of the money changers in the temple and drove them out, so I am coming in these last days to expose and remove the religious spirit that feeds off My Father's house! New music and praise will destroy it.[2] The prophetic word will destroy it. It will flee before My wrath and My praise. I have come to cleanse My house of a

85

religious spirit that has impeded the flow of My presence. There will be cleansing in My house!

"I have sent forth the call and commission to My servants to cleanse My house of a religious spirit. I desire a place of purity. Cast out the religious spirit. As you worship, as you pray, as you prophesy, as you preach, My cleansing waters will wash My people from the chains of religion. They shall be free! Confront the religious spirit. Do not be hindered or intimidated by the fear of man. Move in authority, and be led by My Spirit. Did I not lead My Son to confront the religious spirit that polluted the temple? The victory is already won! The cross has defeated the enemy. Walk in that victory.

"Enjoy Me; praise Me; worship Me! As you dance before Me, you will bring the victory over the religious spirits of intimidation and smothering. Be released to dance before Me in the dance of the Lord Jehovah God."

A Season of Release

"This is a season of great release. Those of My servants who refuse to release what I am doing will be set aside. The river of My presence will be diverted around them, and their ground will be dry. What you release will return to you sevenfold, and in some cases a hundredfold. *No more church as usual!* It is through the release of Spirit-led worship that you shall welcome My presence and invite My glory to come. Declare this truth to My church, and teach this principle to others: My blessing comes when You release My Spirit.

"I demand that worship and prayer be the atmosphere of My house. Begin to set the watchmen in place to pray. I am calling My church to be watchmen's stations, and My people to be wall-dwellers. I am summoning them to take their positions on My prayer wall and fulfill their assignments to watch and pray. There will be twenty-four-hour prayer."

The words of the Lord instantly brought to my mind what had happened the previous Sunday just before the service began. After the worship team had finished praying, as I took my place near the window on the platform, I happened to glance outside. There, perched directly on top of our twenty-foot cross, was a huge hawk. I sensed, at the time, that this was not a coincidence. I knew the Lord was trying to say something to me, but I did not understand what. Now the Lord was revealing to me its significance. The hawk sitting on the cross was a prophetic message.

"Have I not given you a sign?" He said. "Just as I set the hawk on top of the cross to watch, so I am calling the watchmen to watch and intercede for the lost. It is time to push back the curtain of blindness over people. It is time to call the watchmen to their places of intercession on the wall. The harvest is ready."

A Huge Warship

A few days later, as I waited before the Lord, I saw a vision of a huge warship. It was the size of a mighty ocean liner. "What does this mean, Lord?" I asked.

"I am preparing My church," He said. "I am calling forth My people to get on board. The coming storm will not harm those who have signed on for duty and answered My call. I have made every provision. Even now, I am preparing stocks and supplies. My anointing is gracing the workmen.

"My Spirit is fitting the engine room. My Holy Spirit will supercharge this vessel. Nothing will impede its progress. My generals and commanders are staffing the command deck. Rank is coming in My house. The people will know their place. Promotion is also coming quickly. There will be a release of the governing anointing. I will not tolerate rebellion or striving on My ship!

The coming storm will not harm those in God's army.

"My glory will cover the earth as the waters cover the sea, and the ship of My church will move in My glory. I will steer it wherever I desire. It will be a hospital ship for the wounded and sick. It will be a warring vessel for those in captivity. It will be a kingdom ship that brings My government, My righteousness, My peace, and My joy, as it moves mightily through the earth.

"The engine has begun to run. I am about to hoist the anchor, and launch My church into a whole new dimension of ministry. Prepare for the journey. Become familiar with the ship. Get to know the different rooms. Get to know the officers and the troops. Walk among the soldiers and seamen. I want you to know the vessel of My church and its various compartments. In the days to come you will understand why.

"I have a plan and a purpose. What I do in the coming days is very strategic. My strategy builds on sequential events. I do things with divine purpose and intention. What I did yesterday was in preparation for what I do today. From before time until this present moment, and throughout the eons to come, there is a constant progression of My purpose.

"The culmination of one thing is the birthing of the new. The progressions of the waves of My Spirit wash away the debris of the old, establishing the new. With each successive wave, that which has been polluted by the flesh is removed, so that the purity of My purpose can come forth. Deep calls unto deep. The deep of pre-Creation calls to the deep of ultimate fulfillment, and in between are the successive waves of My glory, always moving from deep unto deep.

"You must ride the wave of My glory. It is the energy of My purpose for all of existence. Each wave brings new revelation, understanding, and grace to accomplish My will. Each wave releases new creativity. Each wave prepares the way for the next one. The momentum and size of My purpose-wave is increasing. I am releasing greater power, energy, revelation, and global impact. The successive waves that are coming will sweep over entire continents and global regions. Soon the entire world will be covered by My glory-wave."

The Wave Is Coming

The scene changed, and I saw myself standing on a high mountain where I could see for great distances in every direction. I heard the Lord instructing me to look in all directions. As I turned to look behind me, I saw far in the distance a gigantic wave forming in the ocean. Then I heard the Lord say to me, "Tell My people that My Wave is coming!"

A change was occurring in the heavenlies. Something was transpiring in God's economy and purpose. What happened two days after this

Holy Spirit explosion reaffirmed this awareness in my mind and heart. I was in the city of Hartford, chairing a planning meeting with some other leaders. We were in the process of preparing for a major conference that was scheduled to occur in just a week. Several people had not arrived yet, so I began to share with those who were there what had occurred in our church the previous Sunday.

As I spoke, everyone listened with amazement. In the midst of my testimony, the pastor of the congregation located just down the street from our church entered the room. As he listened to what I was saying, his mouth dropped open, and he said, "This is incredible! The very same thing happened at our church this past Sunday at the very same time it was happening with you. Our entire congregation was swept into heavenly praise and worship for hours. I never did get to preach."

Immediately, we both realized that this was far bigger than any one local church. God was up to something far greater than either one of us could comprehend. This was a God thing! This was not a revival in a local congregation. The Holy Spirit had blown right up our street, and the river of His glory and purpose had inundated both of our churches. This truly was a Holy Spirit explosion. An enormous wave of God's glory is coming!

Chapter Six

A New Level of Prayer

Icons from the past were visible in every direction. Minutely detailed pictures depicting mystical Christians in reverent postures lined the walls of the church. Ancient saints were portrayed in an abstract and surrealistic style. These were not mere portraits; they were holy relics that inspired awe and respect from those who came here to worship. The congregants and the priests would bow their heads and kiss these icons with great reverence. They valued their heritage and the great price that others had paid to live a life devoted to Christ.

The domed ceiling drew my attention upward. Various shades of brilliant colors were projected upon the glistening white, curved surface. These brilliant splashes of light emanated from the many windows that lined the walls of the church. Each window, like a giant slide projector, refracted the beams of light through a mosaic of intricate multi-colored glass, casting its image upon the ceiling. Together, the windows portrayed the gospel story of Jesus' birth, life, crucifixion, and resurrection.

The pews were now occupied by people of all ages who had gathered for the funeral of one of their departed members. Many were dressed in black to mourn the loss of their sister in Christ. I had been invited to participate in the service, since the deceased had been the mother of one of our members. I took a seat in the front pew. The platinum gray casket was positioned in the center of the altar area. I waited respectfully with the others for the service to begin.

The Greek Orthodox priest entered from behind the altar. He was robed in clerical vestments and carried a lantern-shaped censer attached to a long chain. As he approached the casket, the cantors started to sing. The priest stood by the casket and began to wave the censer. As it swung back and forth, smoke filtered out and perfumed the air. This ritual was repeated several times as he made his way completely around the casket.

The pungent incense gradually filled the church. It spread from the altar, past the front rows of seats, until everyone could smell its fragrance. The atmosphere became saturated with this spiritual essence. The effect was total! We were engulfed in the atmosphere of worship. The most powerful source of memory stimulation, the sense of smell, was activated and indelibly linked to this moment. The sensual imagery of this experience lingered with me for several days after the funeral service.

The Atmosphere of God's House

The crisp fragrance of blooming orange blossoms filled the morning air with sweetness. I could feel the tiredness drain from my body, in the warm Sarasota morning sunshine. After months of exhausting activity, we had finally managed to take a few days of vacation. Taking shelter in the shade of the front porch, I finished the last few sips of coffee and lifted my journal to my lap.

I closed my eyes and sought the Lord's presence. Instantly, I could see the scene replayed from a few days before. I was back in the Greek Orthodox church, and I could see the priest swinging the censer. As he waved it, the air moved through it, and incense came forth. The Lord began to speak to me as I recalled this scene.

"The atmosphere of My house is incense," He said. (See Matthew 21:13; I Corinthians 3:16; 6:19.) "The priestly ministry is one of prayer and intercession. My son, just as you saw the priest wave the censer and release perfumed smoke into the air, so I want you to be like that censer—ignited with prayer. This is how the fragrance of prayer will fill My house: My Holy Spirit will blow upon your heart, and your life will become the perfume of prayer.

"I am releasing this new dimension of prayer into My church. I want My people to tend to the priestly ministry. Encourage others around you to enter into the ministry of intercession. I will ignite prayer in My house, and it shall rise to a whole new level. Through priestly prayer I will bring My church into a whole new dimension of intimacy with Me."

Prayer is the means to a new level of intimacy with God.

The Lord's words of instruction caused me to focus my attention upon the censer. What was the Lord saying to me? Why was this so important? If this was so important to the Lord, then I needed to learn more about what He was saying. Intimacy with Him was the cry of my heart, and now He was telling me that prayer was a vital key to greater intimacy.

I immediately turned to the Scriptures. What the Spirit revealed as I began to study God's Word intrigued and fascinated me. I quickly realized that there were three aspects to the use of the censer: the censer itself, the type of incense used, and the person who performed the priestly duty.[1]

The Censer

In Old Testament days, the censer was a metal device used for carrying live coals of fire taken from the altar of the Lord. At the appropriate time, incense was sprinkled upon these live coals. The smoldering incense would fill the place of worship with smoke, and perfume the atmosphere with a sweet fragrance. (See Numbers 16:6, 17–18, 46.)

Most censers were made of bronze and were specifically assigned to individual priests for use in their daily duties. (See Exodus 27:3.) They were flat sheets of metal, probably folded at the corners similar to our modern-day cookie sheet. The fact that the censers of the rebels Korah, Dathan, and Abihu were converted to metal plates to cover the altar confirms this design. (See Numbers 16:38–39.)

The censers used inside the tabernacle were made of pure gold. They were reserved for the burning of incense in the Holy Place on the altar of incense. This duty was performed when the priest went in to trim the lamps every morning, and again when he lit them in the evening. (See Exodus 30:7–8.) Later on, in Israel's worship, Solomon prepared similar firepans of pure gold for the temple. (See I Kings 7:50; 2 Chronicles 4:22.) In Revelation 5:8 and 8:3, 5, the censer appears again. We find the twenty-four elders and the four living creatures holding golden bowls full of incense.

Notice that the closer one's proximity to God's holy presence, the more requirement there is for gold. The tabernacle furniture in the outer court was made of wood and brass. But in the inner court, the candlestick was made of gold, and the altar of incense that stood before the veil was covered with a crown of pure gold. Gold covered the ark of the covenant. The high priest would not dare to enter the Holy of Holies with a brass censer. At a distance from God, the priestly ministry might be performed with a bronze censer, but in God's holy presence, only gold would do!

Once a year, on the Day of Atonement, the high priest entered the Holy of Holies carrying the golden censer. He brought incense from the inner court and threw it upon the burning coals. He held the censer in his hand while the incense burned. The smoke from the firepan rose up and filled the room. It covered the priest's humanity. He was enshrouded in the pure, fragrant incense and veiled from the absolute holiness of God. This cloud of incense protected his life.

> [Aaron] *shall take a firepan full of coals of fire from upon the altar before the LORD, and two handfuls of finely ground sweet incense, and bring it inside the veil. And he shall put the incense on the fire before the LORD, that the cloud of incense*

may cover the mercy seat that is on the ark of the testimony, lest he die.   (Lev. 16:12–13)

The Holy Incense

The initial use of the word *incense* referred to the burning of the fat of rams as a smoked sacrifice or burnt offering. The fat was considered the most valuable part of the animal sacrifice and was completely burned before the Lord, sending up a cloud of wonderfully aromatic smoke similar to that of a barbecue grill. The purpose of this incense offering was to honor God. It so pleased the Lord that He required it: *"In every place incense shall be offered unto my name"* (Mal. 1:11).

The incense used in the tabernacle service was called *"sweet incense"* (Exod. 25:6 KJV), or the "incense of the aromas." The Lord gave the composition of this special incense directly to Moses. It was comprised of a precise mixture of ingredients: stacte, onycha, galbanum, and pure frankincense (Exod. 30:34). These components were carefully mixed according to the craft of the ancient perfumer. Any incense not made within the strict guidelines was rejected as "strange incense."

This sweet incense was reserved exclusively for sacred use. Only the approved priesthood was permitted to use the holy mixture of spices and perfumes as a part of the tabernacle worship of God. Wealthy individuals were sometimes tempted to make their own private supply for personal use. The women of Israel, just like contemporary ladies, loved to perfume their bodies, but were strictly forbidden to use this holy incense as a perfume. If they were caught doing so, the punishment was immediate and harsh: they were to be isolated, or "cut off," from the people.

Despite God's clear warning, the Bible mentions that Israel misused the holy incense in connection with certain pagan worship practices. The worship of Baal, the Queen of Heaven, and other foreign gods by means of incense was strongly condemned by God. (See 1 Kings 11:8–10.) The Lord warned that He would destroy the pagan incense altars. (See Leviticus 26:30; 2 Chronicles 30:14.) He strongly denounced the burning of incense at the pagan shrines on the "high places." (See 2 Chronicles 34:25.) Tragically, Israel disobeyed the Lord regarding the restricted use of incense.

A Symbol of Prayer

The use of incense in Scripture is a clearly identified symbol for prayer. The prayers of the Hebrew people were considered a pleasant aroma offered to God. The psalmist requested that his prayer might be brought before the Lord as incense: *"May my prayer be counted as incense before Thee"* (Ps. 141:2). In the New Testament, the multitudes were praying while Zechariah offered incense. (See Luke 1:10.) The incense used in the heavenly temple is specifically connected, and even identified, with *"the prayers of the saints"* (Rev. 5:8).

Our prayers rise to God just like incense from a censer.

Today, in the life of the church, the true burning of incense is not the actual igniting of a powdered substance. Instead, it is the prayers of the saints lifted before almighty God. It is the body of Christ interceding before His throne.

The Priestly Ministry

The use of the censer and the right to burn incense were special privileges reserved for the sons of Aaron. Each ministering priest was issued his own censer and was carefully taught how to use it properly. Little mention is given to its proper use, though. Instead, the Scriptures chronicle the judgment of God upon those who misused the censer.

Nadab and Abihu

An example of improper use of the censer was when Nadab and Abihu, Aaron's sons, offered *"strange* [or profane] *fire"* before the Lord.

Now Nadab and Abihu, the sons of Aaron, took their respective firepans, and after putting fire in them, placed incense on

*it and offered strange fire before the L*ORD*, which He had not
commanded them. And fire came out from the presence of
the L*ORD *and consumed them, and they died before the L*ORD*.
Then Moses said to Aaron, "It is what the L*ORD *spoke, saying,
'By those who come near Me I will be treated as holy, and
before all the people I will be honored.'" So Aaron, therefore,
kept silent.* (Lev. 10:1–3)

Nadab and his brother Abihu were destroyed in the wilderness of
Sinai because they offered *"strange fire"* before the Lord. We are not sure
exactly what made the fire unacceptable to God. Some scholars speculate
that perhaps it was that Nadab and Abihu rebelled against the authority of Moses and Aaron by presuming to bring an unauthorized offering
before the Lord. If this is the case, the Lord despised their presumptive
action of pride and arrogance. Others surmise that, because the emphatic
prohibition of wine and strong drink was laid upon the priests immediately after this tragedy, the two brothers were performing their priestly
ministry in a drunken condition. Whatever the case may be, their offense
was so abominable that their death is mentioned three times in the
Scriptures. (See Numbers 3:4; 26:61; I Chronicles 24:2.)

Other examples of the misuse of the censer include Korah, Dathan,
and Abiram's challenge of Moses' authority (Num. 16:1–7, 16–24,
31–40); the presumptuous behavior of King Uzziah (2 Chron. 26:3–5,
16–21); and the practices of the seventy elders (Ezek. 8:6–12).

An Angel with a Censer

Thankfully, God does not leave us with a horrible image of spiritual degradation. It is very encouraging, after seeing how far the worship of God had fallen, to turn to the book of Revelation and discover
there the depiction of an angel of God fulfilling the priestly function.
He is holding a golden censer that has been filled with the prayers of
the saints.

*And another angel came and stood at the altar, holding a golden
censer; and much incense was given to him, that he might add it*

to the prayers of all the saints upon the golden altar which was before the throne. And the smoke of the incense, with the prayers of the saints, went up before God out of the angel's hand. And the angel took the censer; and he filled it with the fire of the altar and threw it to the earth; and there followed peals of thunder and sounds and flashes of lightning and an earthquake.

(Rev. 8:3–5)

Incendiary Prayer

It was becoming clear to me why the Lord had reminded me of the Orthodox priest and the smoking censer. He wanted to show me a whole new dimension of prayer. He was using the three elements of the priestly ministry as a beautiful representation of what He desires in our prayer lives. He was teaching me that we are the new order of priests whom He has called to minister in His house. After all, His house is a house of prayer.

But an even more powerful revelation was penetrating my spirit: we are much more than priests. *We are also the golden censers!* We are made pure by His blood and righteousness. He wants us to be the

We are living censers, filled with the glory of God.

pure vessels that He can use in the ministry of intercession. We are human tabernacles, prepared for His habitation. We are *living censers* that contain His glory. As Jesus performs His High Priestly function according to the order of Melchizedek, He takes us in His hands and uses *us* as golden censers. We become instruments of intercession that are available to Him.

His holy fire is within us! This consuming fire is the presence of the Holy Spirit who comes to set our hearts ablaze with God's compassion and power. Just as the angel touched the lips of Isaiah with the white-hot coals from God's altar, setting him on fire (see Isaiah 6:1–7), so Jesus places the coals of fire from the altar, upon our hearts. The same fire that rested upon those gathered in the Upper Room on the

Day of Pentecost now sets us ablaze with God's power and boldness. In our hearts, we carry the red-hot coals from the altar of intercession in the heavenlies. (See Romans 8:26–27.)

But there is one ingredient that is still missing. It is the incense itself! Suddenly, I understood! Prayer is so much more than creating our own mixture of ingredients, then bringing them to God for His response. It is so easy for us to present to Him the burdens and cares of our own lives, instead of discerning what is on His heart, and making that our prayer agenda. We are very good at making "unclean incense." We are often guilty of offering *strange fire* to Him!

True intercession is not presenting to the Almighty a prayer list of the things that have burdened our hearts. True intercession happens when God Himself takes the incense of His own heart and sprinkles it upon the Holy Spirit fire that He has already ignited within the hearts of His saints.

When the Lord Jesus finds a purified vessel He can use as a priestly censer, He ignites the fire of the Holy Spirit within that person. Then He takes some of the incense that He has carried in His own heart and sprinkles it on the coals. The result is an explosion of prayer! The incense bursts into flame and begins to fill the house with the smoke and fire of anointed intercession. The burden of the Lord has now become the prayer of the saints!

In this light, Psalm 37:4 takes on a whole new meaning: *"Delight yourself in the* LORD; *and He will give you the desires of your heart."* Jesus longs for the desires of His heart to become the desires of our hearts. He wants to impart His concerns to us. He wants us to come to the place where we no longer want Him to fulfill the selfish desires of our hearts. Instead, we should long to know the desires of His heart, and to become intercessors that He can use in His priestly ministry. We need to finally surrender our prayer list and submit to His intercessory agenda. There is an appropriate time to present our needs and petitions to the Lord, but He longs for us to get beyond ourselves and begin to serve Him as praying, functioning, Holy Spirit-filled priests.

Let Incense Rise

It was clear to me that prayer and intercession are the keys to entering into a new dimension of intimacy with God. *Surely God knows the desires of my heart,* I thought. *But do I know the desires of His heart?*

The moment this thought entered my mind, I heard Him speak to me again. "Yes, I know your heart's desire. I know that you desire to serve Me. Only your disobedience or rejection can make Me distance Myself from you. That is how much I love you.

"I have given you these days of intimacy with Me because I have some things that I want to teach you. I will reveal secrets to you, which you must know for the days that are coming. I want you to draw close to Me.

"I am pouring out the oil of My compassion and healing. That which I have begun, I will increase. The incense ministry must rise to a new level! My people must enter into a higher dimension of the priestly ministry in My house. Face-to-face fellowship is what I desire.[2] My presence shall fill My house and abide within it."

The words of John the Beloved resounded in my heart:

And when He had taken the book, the four living creatures and the twenty-four elders fell down before the Lamb, having each one a harp, and golden bowls full of incense, which are the prayers of the saints. And they sang a new song, saying, "Worthy art Thou to take the book, and to break its seals; for Thou wast slain, and didst purchase for God with Thy blood men from every tribe and tongue and people and nation. And Thou hast made them to be a kingdom and priests to our God; and they will reign upon the earth." (Rev. 5:8–10)

Truly God desires intimacy with His people. He longs to bring us into a new level of prayer, into the Secret Place with Him.

Part Two

The Well
of His Presence

Chapter Seven

Come to the Well

T he vivid picture appeared so instantaneously that I could have dismissed it as just a passing thought. Had I done so, I would have missed one of the most powerful revelations that the Lord has ever given to me. But experience has taught me to pay close attention to His voice, especially when it comes so spontaneously, without any prompting or effort on my part. I had learned that God often speaks in the form of pictures and images.[1] They flash into our minds seemingly out of nowhere. This is why the Old Testament prophets were called seers; they were able to see what He spoke.[2]

Habakkuk must have been referring to this phenomenon when he wrote,

> *I will stand on my guard post and station myself on the rampart; and I will keep watch to see what He will speak to me, and how I may reply when I am reproved. Then the LORD answered me and said, "Record the vision and inscribe it on tablets, that the one who reads it may run. For the vision is yet for the appointed time; it hastens toward the goal, and it will not fail.*

Though it tarries, wait for it; for it will certainly come, it will not delay." (Hab. 2:1–3)

With the eyes of my spirit, I focused on the scene that the Lord had projected into my mind. At first, the picture appeared like a photographic snapshot, but as I continued to examine it more carefully in the Spirit, more of the scene unfolded. I began to discern the many details that appeared. It was so lucid that what happened next really caught me by surprise. The following words from my journal describe what I saw.

The Vision

A beautiful well appeared with a circular fieldstone wall around its opening. The wall was about three feet high. Two wooden posts were attached to the top of the wall. They extended upward to support a small, peaked roof. This roof provided shade and protection for the well. All around the well were brilliant rays of sunlight. Its water was cool and clear. It beckoned me to draw refreshing water out of its depths.

The scene suddenly changed. I was now looking at an architectural blueprint that depicted a cross section of the same well. The earth had been sliced away in order to reveal the well's interior design and components.

The bottom part of the blueprint, which portrayed the well's characteristics below the surface of the soil, looked more like a geological survey. I could see the entire profile of the well below the ground. The top layer of fertile black soil was carefully marked. Each subsequent layer of soil and stone was clearly visible. The rich soils, and the differing rock textures and formations, made each substratum distinct. These layers served as markers identifying the different levels of depth in the well.

The well penetrated deep into the earth. As it descended, it steadily increased in diameter, widening toward the bottom.[3] Instead of coming to an abrupt end, the bottom of the shaft opened into an underground cavern. A powerful river flowed through the cavern, filling it with an endless supply of fresh water. What at first appeared to be a simple well was actually a means of access to an inexhaustible underground river.[4]

Levels of Revelation

I quickly realized that God had given me this vision of a well in order to teach me something about Himself.[5] Many times the Lord will instruct us through such images. The same God who gave visions to people in Bible times is still giving us visions today—visions that reprove, teach, edify, and empower. I trust that the vision I am about to share will edify and empower you, as well.

Each of the different levels that were identified in this well carried great significance. Each subsequent level represented a different spiritual experience or varying degree of revelation from God. The depth to which you lowered a vessel into the well would determine the nature of what you brought up to the surface.

The water in the well was crystal clear and had no pollution in it whatsoever. The surface of the well represented the "water of salvation." (See Isaiah 12:3.) Many individuals, who were believers in Jesus Christ, had dipped to drink of the water at this entry level. Immediately below this, just under the surface, was a second level identified as "fullness." This depth represented the experience of the baptism in the Holy Spirit. (See Acts 1:8; 19:1–6.) Below this second level were many more and varying degrees of revelation. An inconceivable abundance of God's mysteries and wisdom were hidden in the well.[6]

Very few believers chose to drink from the deeper parts of the well. The wisdom and truth that these individuals received from God were life-giving. They were willing to pay the price in order to reach the deeper levels of revelation. They had labored, investing their time to patiently wait for God's truth to be drawn up from the depths. They were richly rewarded for their investment.

I sensed a deep sadness in the Lord's heart as I pondered what He was revealing to me. His great disappointment was caused by the majority of believers who had rejected His invitation to drink from the depths of the well. Because of their unwillingness and impatience, they refused to draw up truth for themselves. Instead, they chose to drink from the revelation obtained by a small minority of individuals who were willing to pay the price to obtain the deeper water. While the great majority was nourished to a degree by this drink from someone else's cup, they would never know the joy and the sheer delight of drawing the water of revelation out of the heart of God for themselves.

An Invitation to Draw Water

My own heart was broken as I pondered what the Lord was showing me through this vision. *How tragic to ignore such an incredible resource,* I thought. *What a wonderful invitation God has given to us. How sad that we neglect the very thing that can bring us great joy and fruitfulness. What a terrible indictment upon the slothfulness of His people.*

The Lord's voice broke the silence as He confessed the raw truth. "Only those who truly thirst will be satisfied from the depths of My revelation," He said. (See Romans 11:33; Ephesians 3:18–19.) "Enoch was such a person. Enoch chose to abide in the well of My Spirit. He drank deeply of My knowledge. He went beyond the revelation of truth to tap the emotion and very heart of My existence. He chose *Me* beyond My *revelation.* He reached further into the depths of My heart than any other man. He understood My desires and My longing for fellowship. Enoch came to such a great depth in Me that he no longer had any desire to return to the surface.

Intimacy with each of us is God's heart-cry.

"So many of My people have tasted only the top of the well. My son, don't be like those who come only to have their thirst quenched for the moment. Draw deep! Come further down into the depths of My heart. I invite you to draw upon Me. Yes, make a demand upon My resources, My anointing, and My revelation.

"Inquire of Me! This is what Moses did as we spent days together on the mountain. (See Exodus 24:12–18.) This is what My Son did as He walked the earth. (See John 5:19.) He knew how to come to the well to draw from its ocean-like depths. Have I not said, *'Deep calls to deep'* (Ps. 42:7)?

"Above all else, seek intimacy with Me. How I have longed for intimate fellowship with My people! Adam and Eve walked with Me in the place of intimacy. Enoch also walked with Me in the deeper place. There have been others through the ages. But now I invite you to come and draw as others have."

His words pierced through all the clutter of personal agenda and confused motives that so easily cloud our intentions in going to God. He hungers for companionship and fellowship with His people—I sensed this hunger in His plea. Intimacy is His heart-cry! Like a bridegroom searching for His bride, Jesus is longing for intimacy with His church. Allow what He has spoken to me to speak to your heart.

"I am unlocking My secrets," He continued. (See Daniel 2:28.) "I am opening the door of revelation. My truth will break forth. You must strike the rock of revelation in Me. You must labor patiently at the well. It is a wonderful place of intimacy with Me. There is sunlight and truth all around the well. I want to reveal to you the truth that the prophets saw. I desire to release My deeper revelations to My church."

I sensed a sudden change in the tone of His voice. "The time is at hand!" He declared. "In the coming days I will release My truth. Those who wait in My presence shall bring up new truth from the depths of My heart. This fresh revelation shall release entire nations and peoples. Keys of understanding that are needed to unlock strategic doors and solve puzzles and mysteries will be given to those who draw deeply from My well. I will pour My revelation from the depths of My wisdom into those who have yielded their minds and hearts to Me. (See Job 11:7–9.)

"Do not think it strange that I desire to show you many things. Guard what I reveal to you until I have released you to pour it out. In this process of revelation, I will use the water of My truth to cleanse you, heal you, and renew you. (See Psalm 107:20; Ephesians 5:25–27.) I can cause your youth to be restored as you drink from My well. There are many blessings that result in the lives of those who draw from the depths of My well of revelation."

"I want to obey You, Lord. How do I draw up revelation from the well?" I asked. Then God graciously instructed me as to how I could gain greater intimacy with Him.

"Son, you have already begun," He responded. "As you come to Me each day, yield yourself to Me in humility. Allow Me to draw you into My presence. I will take you to places and show you things that will astound you. Relax, and allow yourself to be led by My Spirit. At times, the angels will transport you and accompany you. At other times, you will be taken in the Spirit to see what I will speak to you. Hours will seem like seconds, for in Me time will disappear."

Plumbing the Depths

I was continually more amazed at how the Lord had been speaking to me in my time with Him. He was showing me visions and telling me things that I never could have devised on my own. This was real revelation truth from the heart of God, and it was amazingly part of my daily walk with Him! My heart longed for more of His presence. Every new revelation and every day in God's presence made me yearn for Him even more!

I spoke to Him with even greater conviction: "Lord, I truly desire to draw the truths of life from the depths of Your heart. I am willing to pay the price, Jesus. I am Yours to command. Saturate me with Your presence and Your Word. Draw me into the depths of Your well."

"Son," He responded, "My Word is like a rope that lowers you into the well of My wisdom and revelation.[7] My Word *Through the Scriptures, you will find truth and life.* is a plumb line. It is the means of plumbing the depths of My truth. Stay connected to My Word. I am speaking not only of the Scriptures, but I am also referring to My *logos* (the expression of a thought, concept, or idea) and My *rhema* (the spoken word of God). I speak in many ways.

"My Word is life, and it gives forth life. It heals and delivers; it saves and redeems. My Word brings illumination and revelation. My words are wisdom and understanding. Do you understand how much I desire to communicate with you, and with all My children?

"I will show you great and mighty things that are to come. I will reveal to you that which was from the beginning. My Word and My Spirit speak as one. Dream and vision, prophecy and tongues, are all revelations by My Spirit. I sing My Word to you. I send My Word in night visions and dreams. I speak My Word to you through My prophets and preachers."

Spiritual Words

"O My son, how I long to speak with all My children. How I desire to tell them of My love and mercy. How I long to draw them near to Me and share with them My plans and purposes. But so many refuse to listen. They fill their lives with the clutter and the clanging din of wasted sounds and empty words. If they only knew that just one word from Me would satisfy their hearts and souls beyond measure![8]

"My Word is like spiritual food that releases abundant growth. My Word is the milk of youthful energy; it is the bread of daily sustenance; it is meat for the mature. The apostle Paul understood this. He spoke with spiritual words that brought understanding to his listeners. (See I Corinthians 2:13.) My words are Spirit and life." (See John 6:63.)

The Heart of a Servant

"Too many of My children have their spiritual ears clogged, and their spiritual vision obscured. Their hearts are not right. This is why I have said, *'He who has an ear, let him hear what the Spirit says to the churches'* (Rev. 2:17). The eyes and ears of a true servant are attentive to his master's every move. They are trained to recognize and respond to his needs and wishes. (See Psalm 123:2.) A true servant knows the love and trustworthiness of his master; he does not hesitate to obey! He is sensitive because his heart is right. You must have the heart of a servant.

"A true servant recognizes his master's voice. You must test and judge what you hear. There are many voices. Satan will speak in an attempt to deceive you, but My voice is clearly discerned by My sheep. (See John 10:1–6, 27.) Elijah heard My still small voice despite the wind and the earthquake. I want you to listen as Elijah did. He was able to hear Me whisper. (See I Kings 19:11–13.) If you develop this acute sense of spiritual hearing, you will discern My Word in purity, and you will be able to distinguish it from all the other voices you hear."

The Living Temple

It is so important to discern Your voice, Lord, I thought. *There are so many voices that demand my attention. I really want to hear You whisper, Lord. I don't want You to have to shout to get my attention.*

Truly, the world demands our attention and draws us away from the life-giving well of God's presence. Satan's intention is to fill your ears with so many of the world's voices that you won't be able to hear God's voice—even if He shouts! But why would you continue to listen to the world when the Lord has exactly what you need, all in a calming whisper? His peace and His direction for your life are all in His still, small voice. We must turn our ears toward Him and listen with our hearts and minds focused on Him. This is the path to true intimacy with Him! This is the way in which He reveals Himself to us.

"Open my ears to hear Your voice accurately, Jesus," I prayed, longing for that intimacy.

"My voice is in My Spirit," He answered. "I have sent Him as the One who reveals. He is the anointing that illuminates; He is the Golden Candlestick that gives light; He is the Revelator. He hovered over the darkness and brought light when I spoke. He brooded over the deep waters and formed matter. He is pure and holy! He releases revelation and understanding. His presence is with you and in you. He will direct your thoughts and teach you about Me. I have sent Him to reveal My Son to the church. (See John 16:13.)

"My Holy Spirit is easily quenched, and does not impose Himself upon you. Only the yielded individual will hear and discern His voice. He is like the wind; you cannot tell where He comes from or where He is going, but you can readily discern when He is present. (See John 3:8.)

"You are the living temple of the Holy Spirit. Your physical body is the outer court of the temple. Your soul is the inner court. The soul realm consists of your mind, will, and emotions. Your spirit is the holy place.

110

Your spirit is the candle of the Lord; it is the inner sanctuary where I dwell. I manifest My presence in your spirit, and from your spirit-man I illuminate your understanding. My presence within you releases My light into your life. *'The spirit of man is the lamp of the LORD, searching all the innermost parts of his being'* (Prov. 20:27)."

Spirit to Spirit

I sat perfectly still, totally engrossed in conversation with the Lord. My spirit was responding just like the candle He referred to. The slightest hint of His breath moved me deep within. His gentlest whispered word made a distinct impression in my spirit. All along, the vision of the well remained fixed in my mind as He spoke into the depths of my being by His Spirit.

God manifests His presence in many different ways.

"Communion with Me takes place within your spirit," He continued. "Dialogue with Me is Spirit to spirit. This method of communication bypasses the soul realm. The revelation of My truth within your spirit is manifested from your spirit into your mind, and sometimes even into your physical body. My thoughts and words are not dependent on your mind or emotions.[9]

"You must learn to respond to Me in your spirit-man. This is what happened when Mary and Elizabeth first encountered each other after they both had become pregnant. John leaped within Elizabeth's womb when Mary drew near. John's spirit was responding to My presence within Mary. It was a spirit-to-Spirit encounter. John was responding to the witness of the Holy Spirit moving within him. (See Luke 1:39–41.)

"The two men who walked with Me on the road to Emmaus had a similar experience. At first, they were unaware of who I was because I had blinded their spiritual eyes. But the words that I spoke to them were spiritual words, and they entered into their spirits. During the intimate moments when we communed together through the breaking of bread, the revelation of who I was dawned upon them. Their spiritual eyes were instantly opened. They immediately understood why their hearts had burned within them as I spoke about the Scriptures. Their spirits were bearing witness of My presence. (See Luke 24:13–35.)

"My presence can also be discerned by recognizing the manifestations that come in the physical realm. Your physical body will respond to My presence in very definite ways. You may experience intense heat or smell the fragrance of My presence or hear the sound of wind. Sometimes, you will not be able to remain standing because My glory will overwhelm you. You may also find yourself overcome with emotion because of My presence within you. You may laugh, weep, or travail with great compassion. Learn to recognize and discern all these manifestations of My presence.

"My Holy Spirit enables your mind to receive and process My revelation. This is how truth, mystery, prophecy, and divine secrets are made known to the conscious mind. There is an invisible prophetic river that continually flows in the spiritual realm. When you prophesy, you tap into this river. I invite you to come to the well of My presence so that you may receive deeper prophetic revelation. I want you to know that the well of My Spirit is inexhaustible. Tap into My Spirit, and allow Him to breathe upon you. I am Spirit, and I am Truth."

The Lord paused for a moment, then spoke once more with great feeling. "My heart rejoices because I know that your desire is for intimacy with Me." Indeed, God rejoices with each of His children when they meet with Him in the Secret Place.

The Meeting Place

The picture of the well was indelibly etched upon my spirit. In these few moments, it had become more than merely an image or a vision to me. It was a special place in the spiritual realm where all the Lord's people are invited to come to commune with Him, to draw from the deeper waters of revelation in His Spirit. It is far more than the well of salvation; it is the well of His presence! How wonderful to know that we are invited to draw from its depths.

I knew that this was the place where I would come to spend time with Him in the days ahead.[10] Revelation, mystery, and truth were all waiting to be discovered in the well. Even more important was the knowledge that He would be waiting there to commune with me. What joy and delight filled my heart and soul! He awaits all of us at the well of His presence!

Chapter Eight

Choose Intimacy

T he ancient priest stood before the brazen laver, gently washing himself in the sacred pool of water. He stared intently into the mirrorlike surface, noting every detail of his reflection. He saw beyond the furrowed lines of age and experience that the years had indelibly carved upon his face. He was searching his soul. His tears of repentance fell into the pool, creating gentle ripples that slowly faded into the surface and disappeared. He knew that this was more than a ritual cleansing. He was preparing to enter into God's presence. His heart must be pure! This was a life-or-death issue. (See Exodus 30:17–21; 40:7.)[1] Self-examination before God was an absolute necessity. Finally, he straightened himself, then dried his face and hands with a linen towel that had been draped carefully over his shoulder. There was an innocence and purity about him that had not existed moments before. He turned from the laver and quietly stepped through the curtain into the Holy Place.

I stood before the well of God's presence much as the ancient priest had stood before the sacred laver. Even though centuries had passed, the still surface of the spiritual water before me served a similar purpose. My life was reflected, and all my weaknesses and humanity lay exposed before me. *This must be how David felt,* I thought, *when God sent the prophet to expose his sinful heart.* The following is the scene from Israel's history. (See 2 Samuel 12:1–9.)

Exposing the King's Sin

Nathan's discerning eyes flashed with prophetic judgment as he stood before the king of all Israel. His finger pointed directly into David's face with an accuracy that forbade denial. David knew that there was no place to hide. The trusted prophet's words came like nails hammered into the cross of a common criminal. They announced his guilt and shame. *"You are the man!"* (2 Sam. 12:7), Nathan said without wavering.

The events of the past months played out on the screen of David's mind. His passionate lust for Bathsheba that could not be denied, the unwanted pregnancy, the plot that succeeded in the murderous death of Uriah—they were all like successive scenes that revealed his evil heart.

The charade was finally over. David's sin against God lay exposed before the nation and the world. Every generation to come would know that he was an adulterer and a murderer despite all his successes. But for David there would be no more hiding and deception. He was free at last from the tormenting guilt that was destroying him on the inside. Out of his painful anguish, David openly confessed his sin to God. The price of his failure was costly, but God's mercy prevailed. (See 2 Samuel 12:13–23.)

David's most valued possession was intimacy with God. His sin had put him in jeopardy of losing his relationship and closeness to the Lord. His agonizing prayer of confession and repentance reveal this man's unrelenting passion for God's presence:

Have mercy on me, O God, according to your unfailing love; according to your great compassion blot out my transgressions. Wash away all my iniquity and cleanse me from my sin. For I know my transgressions, and my sin is always before me.

Against you, you only, have I sinned and done what is evil in your sight, so that you are proved right when you speak and justified when you judge. Surely I was sinful at birth, sinful from the time my mother conceived me. Surely you desire truth in the inner parts; you teach me wisdom in the inmost place. Cleanse me with hyssop, and I will be clean; wash me, and I will be whiter than snow. Let me hear joy and gladness; let the bones you have crushed rejoice. Hide your face from my sins and blot out all my iniquity. Create in me a pure heart, O God, and renew a steadfast spirit within me. Do not cast me from your presence or take your Holy Spirit from me.

(Ps. 51:1–11 NIV)

Search Me, O God

David's words resounded in my own heart as I began to pray. "Lord Jesus, I quiet myself in Your presence today. Please cleanse me of anything that would hinder my intimacy and communion with You. I desire a pure heart and unselfish motives. I know that my heart is deceptive and wicked, and I am no different from King David or any other man. (See Jeremiah 17:9.)

David had an unrelenting passion for God's presence.

"You know the hidden things, and nothing is concealed from Your view. My prayer today is the same as David's.

Search me, O God, and know my heart; try me and know my anxious thoughts; and see if there be any hurtful way in me, and lead me in the everlasting way.   (Ps. 139:23–24)

His response confirmed my feelings of impurity. "My son," He replied, "there can be no pretense or deception when you come into My presence. You must come with a clean heart. My Spirit guards the entrance into My presence, and He will require absolute honesty and transparency from all who approach Me. (See Jeremiah 17:10; Romans 8:27; Revelation 2:23.) He will search your heart and wash you spiritually with My Word."

All My Fears Are Dissolved

Instantly, the Holy Spirit began to expose my hidden fears. (See Ephesians 5:13–14.) Things that I had struggled with for years came rushing into my conscious thoughts. "There are so many fears that I struggle with, Lord," I admitted. "Fear of failure, poverty, shame, sickness, death, rejection, and criticism all harass me. Insecurity seems to continually haunt me and compel me to search for my true identity. Lord, only You have the answer to my dilemma."

He reassured me of His mercy. "My son, don't you see that all your fears are dissolved when you come to the well of My presence? Drinking from My well is the secret. Many people pass by My well. Some never taste of the life-giving water of My Spirit. Others taste and discover that I am good. But oh, My son, the real joy is in drinking deeply. In the depths of My presence, your cares and concerns are resolved. Once you have begun to drink of My well, no other source can satisfy you."

The oppression of my worries and anxieties began to lift. A few moments in His presence was all it took to set me free from these crippling fears, and it will do the same for you. The words of Scripture echoed in my heart: "[Cast] *all your care upon Him, for He cares for you*" (1 Pet. 5:7 NKJV). He was actually caring for me with tender mercy and love. His heart is full of love for all His children.

"I want you to come to My Well every day," He said. "I will cleanse you, and then I will direct you to the specific level from which I would have you drink on each occasion. The needs and demands of the moment will determine where I enable you to draw revelation from the depths of My Spirit."

Each Person Is a Vessel

As He continued, I could sense the Lord speaking as a Father about His care and concern for every one of His children. I hope that you will sense this, too.

"Those who come to draw from the well of My presence are like many different vessels. Each life has been fashioned by Me. (See Isaiah

64:8.) I have designed every individual expressly to carry My anointing, and to fulfill a unique purpose. When his life is filled with the living water of My Spirit, he is empowered to accomplish My will for his life.

"When My children draw from My well, some individuals have learned to draw up truth in abundance. These are the ones whom I have used to release the revelation of My truth into My church. Salvation by faith, the priesthood of all believers, baptisms, healing, My outpouring of Pentecostal power, grace and not law, the evangelistic calling, the teacher and pastor, and more recently, the prophet and apostle—these are only a few of the truths that have been released from the well of My presence. These revelations have brought restoration and release to My church.

"I intend to reveal My Father-heart to My church. In the days to come, a fresh revelation of Fatherhood will be released from My well. My kingdom government and purposes in these last days will also be revealed in greater measure. The knowledge of this impending revelation causes the enemy to tremble. He is aware that his time is limited."

Sealed in the Well

"There are certain levels of revelation in the well of My presence that are inaccessible. (See I Corinthians 2:7, 10.) These are the things that have been sealed. They can be opened only at the time determined by the Father, and then only to those who are ordained *A fresh revelation* to carry them out. Some of these truths have to *of God's heart is* do with the nations; others have to do with judg- *being released* ment; still others have to do with the mysteries of *to the church.* the coming ages and eons. These things are still locked in the heavenly vaults of revelation. (See Acts 1:7.)

"These are days of great revelation! My Spirit is moving mightily through the earth. The prophets are alive with My presence as My Spirit is revealing My purpose to them. My church is about to explode! The earth will be covered with My grace and judgment.

"You must make a demand upon Me. You must draw up revelation truth out of My heart. When My servant John was on the Isle of Patmos, he made a demand upon My anointing. He was in the Spirit on the Lord's Day. (See Revelation 1:10.) As he sought Me, I gave great vision and revelation to him. I will do the same for you and for all those who will seek Me now."

Do you hear what God is saying to you? If you will seek His face, He will give divine revelation to you. He will reveal not only Himself, but also His plans for you and for the church. You may be called upon to give a message to the church. Seek the Lord today, and begin to draw truth from His well of revelation.

Waiting at the Well

I hungered for this revelation knowledge to be made known immediately, but My eagerness provoked impatience within me. *I will make a demand upon Him*, I thought. *I will draw up the revelation of His purpose.* My intentions were good, but my heart was wrong. His instructions brought immediate correction to my impatience.

"You must learn how to come to the well of My presence. When You come to My well, *wait* upon Me. (See Psalm 27:8, 14; 63:1; Isaiah 40:31.) This will allow Me to bring truth from the depths of the well. Sometimes, waiting means to be silent and to express quiet worship and devotion. At other times, waiting upon Me means to dance and shout and twirl about. There are many ways to approach Me. It is not just in your quiet time as we walk together, but it is also in the times of worship when I come to My church in glory and in the cloud of My presence. (See Exodus 40:34–38.) Draw near to Me then, as well.

"Sometimes you will discover that you are at the well of My presence in the midst of corporate worship. You must draw from the well of revelation glory in that moment. Learn to recognize My presence, and press into Me regardless of the time, place, or circumstances. I will teach you to draw from the well at all times and in every season. It is My desire and joy to show My children how to draw from the well of My presence."

The word *wait* flashed before me as a terrible warning from the Lord. I was His servant; He was not mine. It was His prerogative to release revelation knowledge in His own way and time. I needed to learn to wait upon Him.

The Results of Disobedience

As the Lord continued, He redirected my attention. "My son, I want you to take careful notice of what is growing around the well of My presence."

The vision of the well reappeared before me. As I examined the well, I could see myriad plants, shrubs, and trees growing around its perimeter. It quickly became obvious to me that this conglomeration of plants was not intended to be there and had not been planted by the Lord. In certain places, the tangle of growth was so thick that access to the well was almost impossible. I pondered how these plantings had come to exist so close to the well.

"Do you see all of these plants and trees that grow by the well?" He asked. "There are many varieties of vegetation—trees, creeping vines, and tall grass. Weeds have also grown up, and briars and thistles have made access to Me very difficult where it was once simple. All these different growths are the result of disobedience. They have been planted here and nurtured by those who have tasted of My revelation, then used it for their personal gain. (See Acts 20:30.)

"Much of this growth is the result of individuals who have received revelation from Me. They have walked in that revelation truth, releasing it to multitudes through their ministry and example, or by their prophecy and teaching. I have greatly anointed some of these individuals, and many have performed confirming miracles, signs, and wonders in My name. But the time came when they ceased to drink from My well. They began to depend upon the level of revelation truth and anointing they had already received. They became planted beside the well. This should not have been so. They stopped short of My purpose.

"The growth that you see around the well is the end result of their disobedience. These plants have a measure of life in them, but they often hinder My people from true intimacy with me. They typify many of the various movements, organizations, and cults that exist today. They were created as a result of revelation, but many have stopped growing; some even inhibit or prevent intimacy with Me.

"My purpose has often been hindered because those who have drawn from the well of My presence have diverted My truth and anointing in order to water their own fields. They have used My truths to irrigate and nurture their own visions and goals. Their hearts have turned from My presence. Instead of seeking continued intimacy and communion with Me, they have chosen to stop at the point of revelation and have become planted by the well. Their closeness to the well is deceptive. There was truth in them in the beginning, but that truth is no longer alive.

"This tendency is what prompted Peter's desire to build three tabernacles on the Mount of Transfiguration. (See Matthew 17:1–8.) He wanted to abide in the revelation truth instead of realizing that My glory and presence are the true reality. My heart is saddened because so many have come to the well to draw up truth and revelation, but have chosen to turn away from intimacy with Me.

"Many have come to the well, not for the water it contains, but for the fruit and vegetation that surround it. They have tasted My truth from the lives of others, but have never learned to drink of the well for themselves. They have a measure of understanding, but many times it is polluted because of the selfish motives of those who would market My revelation for personal gain. Instead of pointing people to the well of My presence, they draw attention to the revelation that they have received and make themselves the source of truth. Whenever this happens, My heart is grieved.

God's glory and His presence are the true reality.

"All revelation is given to release life and draw men to Me. My desire is to have many sons and daughters who will come into communion with Me. I long for My bride to come to Me, not for what I can do or reveal to her, but for who I am. (See Matthew 25:1–13.)

"O My son, don't be like so many others. Your mind, will, and emotions can cripple My flow and stifle intimacy with Me. Your flesh can seduce you into serving selfish interests. When this happens, weeds and thorns begin to grow among the fruit of revelation truth, and My will and purpose are thwarted and often misdirected. I desire purity, not mixture. Don't settle for life *near* the well of My presence. Rather, come close and partake of it! Choose Me, son, above all else."

His Word Thunders

The Lord was relentless, insisting on purity of motive in the lives of those who seek Him. "When there is pure, unhindered communion, and your motive is to simply be with Me, then that which is produced in your life is like the Tree of Life, whose leaves are for the healing of the nations. (See Revelation 22:2.) The truth that you receive in My presence produces life. The spiritual words of revelation that are spoken out of the place of intimacy and communion with Me have the power to heal entire nations, cultures, tribes, and peoples. They bring healing and deliverance to those who hear and receive them. They shatter and sever chains of bondage and sin. They are sharp and powerful, alive and active." (See Hebrews 4:12.)

The Lord's speech deepened into a pulsating resonance of divine, omnipotent authority as He continued to explain His intentions. "I am preparing to release My Word to the nations. It will come out of the depths of My presence. It will thunder through the earth. Prison doors will be opened. Nations will shake. Just as Moses spoke out of My presence with My authority, and Egypt reeled under My power and judgment, so I am releasing a new sound in the earth.

"My Word shall break forth from My apostles and prophets who have come to the well of My presence. They have spent time with Me. They have chosen to turn aside from their normal activities and mundane cares. They have ceased church life as usual and have sought My face. They have gathered at the well of revelation to remove the stone that has covered its entrance and prevented My church from receiving My Word. (See Genesis 29:8.) Not only will My sheep be watered, but the ultimate purpose of My creation will be fulfilled. My Word will accomplish what I send it to do!" (See Isaiah 55:11.)

The force of His words shook my entire body. There was no doubt that He was preparing to unleash a powerful revelation of His ultimate, cataclysmic purpose into the earth.

Knowledge or Intimacy

Silence spread over Him—a deep, brooding silence that, although inaudible to the human ear, seemed deafening in the Spirit. I wanted to say something, but dared not, knowing it would be totally inappropriate. Gradually the austere silence dissolved into a peaceful, softening tenderness that blanketed Him like the robe of a bridegroom preparing to meet His bride. He had more to say to His church.

"Do not allow your soul and spirit to be polluted by this world's distractions," He said lovingly. "Do not let the desires of the flesh tempt you to settle at the present level of revelation you have received. My desire is for you, and others whom I have called, to be open channels through which My truth can flow. Open your heart to Me. It is not a question of your being usable to Me. It is a question of how much you are yielded, obedient, and intimate with Me.

"In the Garden, Adam and Eve walked with Me. We had fellowship, and our walks together in the cool of the day gave great joy to Me. But they chose knowledge over intimacy. Then came Enoch. He was one of the few who chose intimacy rather than insight. His heart was pure. Noah was also close to Me in a time when all men's hearts were corrupt. Moses, My servant, chose Me out of his weakness. (See Exodus 33:12–15.) Elijah was one who desired communion with Me and knew how to drink of the well of My presence. Like Moses, he did not want to go on in life if I did not accompany him.

"On the Mount of Transfiguration, Moses and Elijah appeared with Me. Their relationship with Me uniquely qualified them to be there. The glory of My presence and the joy of intimacy with Me were their heart-cry. They represented the law and the prophets, which both speak of closeness with Me. The law leads to Me, and the prophetic anointing draws mankind to Me.

"Do you see that the revelation from the well of My presence is meant to draw all mankind to Me? The Holy Spirit's work is to reveal Me! That is why you must come into My presence, spirit *Even the angels* to Spirit. Those whom I use the most understand *don't have the* this simple truth. Give Me your heart and your *intimacy you can* devotion. Give Me your attention and your ear. *have with God.* Let us be lovers and friends. Eternity awaits us. Even the angels desire, but cannot have, what only My bride and I will enjoy."

By now I had formed a picture of Him as He spoke with me. It seemed as though His arms were raised and outstretched in a beckoning gesture as He spoke.

"You must choose whether you will be like those who come only for truth and revelation, or those who come primarily to be with Me. If you choose Me, then indeed, life-giving truth, soul-saving power, *dunamis*[2] power will be released as you draw from the well of My presence.

"It is out of sweet communion in the well of My presence that life flows—not in the truth itself. Truth sets you free, but My presence gives you life. Only as you abide in Me do you have life."

He paused and breathed deeply. "Choose life." He sighed, paused again, and whispered a final plea. "Choose intimacy with Me."

His voice softened to an almost inaudible level; every word was pregnant with feeling. The intensity of His gaze totally arrested me. His eyes were full of longing. They sparkled with moisture, and a single tear coursed down His right cheek and fell upon His robe, a sign of His passionate longing for intimacy with His bride.

A Vision of the Spirit

I was so moved by the Lord's deep longing for intimacy with His bride that it took several minutes before I could regain my composure. My emotions were loosed, and everything within cried out for intimacy with Him.

After several minutes, the intensity of His words diminished. I sensed that there was more He wanted to teach me, so I sat before Him, quietly waiting. Suddenly a delightful scene appeared, and I was seated atop a galloping horse, riding along an ocean beach in the brilliant sunshine. The beautiful white stallion I was riding had no saddle or bridle. Its muscles flexed effortlessly and rippled with great strength. Unrestrained freedom permeated every fiber of its being. I felt such a sense of power, excitement, and adventure. The water sprayed around us as the majestic steed galloped ahead through the shallow waves, his hooves propelling splashes of rainbow-colored mist in every direction.

The horse's freedom to run at will made me fearful at first, but I soon realized that I was safe and could trust the horse to take me wherever he wanted without harm. We were covering great spaces of distance in only seconds. I was being transported from one place to another rapidly, and entire sections of beach were traversed in an instant. Then the Lord spoke.

Letting Go

"The white horse represents My Spirit. You must trust My Spirit to carry you where I want to take you. There are no reins, because if there were, you would attempt to steer. You must trust the Spirit. You need to be abandoned to Me and trust Me. You have always felt the need to be in control. I am calling you to release control to Me.

"Those who yield to My Spirit walk in an anointing that enables them to live without manipulating their circumstances and lead without controlling other people. They are Spirit-led. True spiritual authority flows out of submission and obedience to Me. When you take the reins, you put control in your hands, and your mind and flesh take over. When I am in control, then your thoughts and actions are inspired and graced by Me."

Exploring New Spiritual Territory

"The different locations along the beach are the situations of life in which you find yourself. I desire to move you into new places and introduce you to new things. My will is to break the tendency you have to be comfortable and to dwell in the familiar. If you will yield to My Spirit, you will move with ease and joy into the new situations and experiences that I have planned for you. I want to set you free. Where My Spirit is, there is liberty. (See 2 Corinthians 3:17.)

"You must allow Me to give you the ability of multiple focus. I am a big God, but when you seek to control the reins, you limit your ability to embrace a greater dimension of My revelation. Trust Me! Trust My Holy Spirit. Each day will bring new opportunities and new environments of My revelation."

I watched the vision unfolding before my eyes as if it were a suspenseful movie. I did not know what to expect, but I was certainly enjoying the ride. I had no control over what would happen next. Abruptly, the white stallion I was riding turned inland, away from the white, sandy beach. The roar of the breakers faded as he galloped along a narrow trail that led into thick, pine woodlands. I heard the Lord say, "There will be times when I will lead you to explore inland in order to scout out new territories of truth and revelation. Do not get attached to the land you pass through. Stay on the horse of My Spirit, because there are many places of revelation and experience I would lead you through. (See Psalm 32:8; Acts 8:29; 16:6–7; Romans 8:14.) There may be times when we will pass through a place of exploration in the Spirit, then leave it, only to return later with new insights with which to explore it further. This is the method I use to teach My servants and instruct them in My ways.

"Let My Holy Spirit teach you. (See John 14:26; 16:13.) Allow Him to lead you where I have instructed Him to take you. There are many things that you must learn; and if you take control and try to steer, you will miss the paths of revelation I have ordered for you. This will cause you to lose precious time. You will have to backtrack to make up for your lack of understanding because you missed the path."

Soaked in Revelation

"I will draw you by My Spirit into the well of My presence. My Holy Spirit will direct you to the level of revelation truth that is to be given to you on any specific day or in a certain season. Allow yourself to be immersed in the spiritual depth to which My Spirit takes you. Be saturated in the sights, sounds, smells, and words of that environment. Drink deeply of the water of revelation in that setting. This is how I instruct My servants. I call them by My Spirit into the well of My presence. I direct them to the level of revelation from which I would have them drink. It is not for you to decide what depth to draw from.

Let your entire being be saturated by God's revelation glory.

"Sometimes I would have you draw from the same level in the well for many days. You must drink deeply of the revelation that you receive from that level. Let it fill your soul and spirit. Let it overflow your vessel. Be so filled that you become soaked in My revelation truth. Let your entire being be saturated by My revelation glory.

"By doing this, you will *become* the revelation truth. My purpose is for you to become the truth, not just to know or have the truth. The word of revelation must become flesh. Blessed is he who hears and does the things I reveal by My Spirit. (See Matthew 7:24–27.) Being in My presence will transform you!"

The Well and the River

"The mysteries of creation, life, and eternity contained within the well of My presence are not stagnant and unmoving. My well is a place that accesses a mighty spiritual river. This river flows unseen, yet those who have spiritual eyes and vision know that it exists. It is the river of My prophetic revelation and presence. It is the place of intimacy with Me.

"Was it not at the well of Jacob that I spoke to the Samaritan woman about the existence of a hidden source of living water? (See John 4:1–26.) I told the woman that I knew the source of this veritable fountain springing up into everlasting life. I said that all who drink from this source would never thirst. I encouraged the woman to ask Me for this living water.

"I invite you to ask Me for living water from the well of intimacy with Me. The well of My presence is the place of access to My great river of living water. This is why I said that if you drink of My Spirit, out of your belly shall flow rivers of living water (John 7:38). Once you begin to drink of this source, you will become a channel through which My living water can flow to others. This fountain is the true source of life."

Times of Rest

In the Spirit, the vision continued to unfold as the Lord narrated each scene. The youthful stallion periodically slowed to a stroll and stopped to drink or to graze contentedly. I was forced to sit patiently atop him, and wait until he decided to move on.

The Lord said, "There are times when My Spirit will bring you to a place of rest. Do not be concerned. Rest in Me, and learn to trust My Holy Spirit's direction. There are seasons of slower progress, and even complete stillness in Me."

This came as a welcome relief. I knew that there would be so much to learn and process that times of rest and reflection would be very important.

The Choice Still Remains

The vision faded, and I sat quietly in my study, reflecting on the words of the Lord. *Things really haven't changed much since the Garden of Eden,* I thought. *Adam and Eve had to choose between communion with God or the knowledge of good and evil. The option for contemporary believers is intimacy with God or revelation knowledge. Of which tree should we eat?* I wondered. *The choices remain the same!*

Should I yield to the leading of the Holy Spirit and let go of the reins of control, or should I determine my own course in life? All my questions were redundant. The answer was obvious. What could possibly be more valuable than intimacy with Him? Even the knowledge of good cannot compare to being in His presence.

An audience with Him requires a pure heart, I acknowledged. (See Psalm 24:3–4.) *I dare not presumptuously approach His holy presence without careful self-examination.* I had been forewarned that the Holy Spirit guards the way into His presence. *But the Word of the Lord is available to wash and cleanse my heart and prepare me to enter into His presence,* I reassured myself. *I need to be careful to wash in the laver of His Word before approaching His holy presence.* (See Ephesians 5:26.)

Deep love and reverence filled my heart as I bowed my head and began to pray. "You are the most important person in my life, Lord," I uttered with genuine sincerity. "With all my heart I say, 'I love You.' Your fellowship is sweet, and Your companionship is beyond comparison. All else pales in the light of Your presence.

"I really desire to drink from Your well. Draw me into the depths of Your presence, Lord. No other source will satisfy me! Lord, I choose You above all else. I choose intimacy!"[3]

Chapter Nine

Walking with Jesus

For months I had been enjoying wonderful intimacy with the Lord. The invisible spiritual realm was incredibly real to me, and the well of His presence continually beckoned me to come and walk with God. I did not have to struggle or wait for hours to gain a sense of His presence. I would simply recall the vision of the well that He had given me. I was able to approach it in the Spirit. He was always waiting there to meet me.

I would plunge myself into the well of His presence, and the Holy Spirit would draw me into its depths. I felt myself being lowered into the crystal-clear water. God's presence and light encompassed me. Whenever I arrived at the place of revelation He planned to give to me that day, the Holy Spirit would usher me out of the well at that level. It was like riding a spiritual elevator into the depths of God's wisdom and knowledge. Each level contained different mysteries to explore and revelations to learn.

On one particular occasion, as the Holy Spirit drew me into intimacy with the Lord, I found myself stepping from the well onto a worn pathway. I did not realize it at that moment, but this was the beginning of an incredible visionary journey in the Spirit that would eventually lead me into the very throne room of heaven. It is my prayer that this extensive vision will minister to you and show you the heart of God as you've never seen it before.

Jesus Opened the Book

Jesus was waiting for me beside the well-trodden pathway, and we began to walk through the countryside together. We were strolling through a large open area. Off to my right, in the distance, I could see a beautiful, expansive valley. I had such peace and rest in my spirit. I felt a gentle urging to turn and explore the valley—it was so enticing—but I suppressed it, and we continued on.

The Lord was carrying a book that had the appearance of a personal journal. He stopped in the middle of the pathway and examined the book, holding it in both of His hands. Then He carefully opened it to a specific page that was identified by a bookmark. The open pages of the journal appeared to contain lessons and instructions for the walks that we were taking together. I was surprised to discover that the marker had been placed in the book precisely where we had concluded our last walk.

He pondered the page for a moment, then looked at me. There was such love and compassion in His eyes; they spoke to me without a word ever being uttered. He reached out His hand and gently placed it on my shoulder. I could feel His love and kindness. With that single touch, I felt my spirit being washed and refreshed.

"My son, I am so pleased that you have come to walk with Me," He said. "More than teaching you or revealing My mysteries to you, I want to be with you today. Please let Me share Myself with you. I care about you, and I love you. I yearn to be with you just as much as you need and desire to be with Me.

God yearns to be with you as much as you need to be with Him.

"I long to talk with all My sons and daughters. I love to speak with My little ones. (See John 21:15; Acts 20:28.) Those who come to Me with childlike simplicity are so delightful to Me. Their spirits are so open and ready to be with Me. (See Mark 10:13–16.) They are satisfied to come and simply play in My presence. The only demand that they make is for My full attention. That brings Me great joy. I am blessed by their pure motives."

His face mirrored the joy in His heart as He spoke. A broad smile graced His countenance.

"I could teach you much today from My Book of Mysteries," He continued, "but what would you rather I do—give you My attention, or give you My teaching and revelation?"

"Lord, You are more important to me than anything else," I responded. "My desire is to be with You. Just to be in Your presence is enough! I am so honored that You would take this time to spend with me. I love You so much."

Beams of Light

As I followed a pace behind Him, the Lord walked to the side of the pathway and sat down in the cool shade of a sprawling oak tree. He motioned with His hand, and I took a seat facing Him on a nearby rock. Sunlight filtered through the canopy of leaves and danced upon the grass-covered earth.

I noticed several large boulders and stones nearby. An unexplainable, ominous sense of fear suddenly began to overtake me. It seemed to be emanating from the boulders just a short distance away. A cold chill spread throughout my body, and I shivered with the sense that an evil presence was lurking there. I glanced toward Jesus and looked directly into His eyes, seeking comfort and security. I was shocked by what I saw. His eyes were pure white. There were no pupils or any normal distinguishing characteristics of the human eyes. Instead, an absolutely pure, radiant white light shone from them. (See John 8:12.) I could not bear to look at this incredible brilliance.

I was filled with confusion and turmoil. There was a war going on inside me. A great evil force was obviously coming against me from the enemy. He definitely did not want me to look directly into Jesus' eyes. I realized that if I were to do this, the brilliant light would penetrate deep into my soul and spirit and expose any evil desire or sin within me. (See I Corinthians 4:5; I John I:5–10.) The enemy was trying to force me to hide the evil within my own life from Jesus.

Jesus began to speak. His voice was firm and reassuring. "My son, I have known all along what is in your heart. You cannot be in My presence or look upon My face without exposing your flesh and your soul. You must understand that Satan would like you to draw back from Me. He knows that if you look into My eyes, you will become a pure vessel. Then he will have lost ground in your life." (See John 3:17–21; Ephesians 5:8–14.)

As Jesus spoke, brilliant shafts of light shone forth from His eyes. Wherever He looked, these streams of light followed like beams from a searchlight or lighthouse. They were so brilliant that even in the bright midday sun they were easily discernible. Nothing could hide from His supernatural vision. No one could prevent this light from penetrating into the very interior of his or her being. (See Ephesians 5:13.) As He turned His head, the beams of light moved. Even the rocks and trees became transparent as the beams from His eyes passed by them. The light penetrated right through them, revealing their interior composition, like an X ray.

Then the light flashed upon me. I felt totally exposed; my soul was naked before Him. It would have been useless to try to cover my nakedness or hide my sinfulness. The light from His eyes penetrated into the very depth of my being. I fell to my knees, captured by the brilliant, pure radiance of His all-seeing stare.

"Son, I am cleansing your life," He said. "I am bringing wholeness to you in every way. The things that lie ahead require purity of heart and motive. I am doing a purifying work in you. The truths I am about to reveal from My Book of Mysteries will require you to walk in a level of purity and holiness that you have not yet attained. That is why I hesitated today as I opened the book. That is why I have come with the light of My presence. I know that if I reveal any more mystery and revelation from the well of My presence to you before I cleanse your heart, it will destroy you.

"I must cleanse your life so that in the days to come, you will be able to receive the truth and revelation that proceed from My Secret Place. I want to bring you into the heavenly realms, yes, even into My strategy room, but you cannot come in the flesh; you must come only in the spirit."

Jesus turned to take a seat, and the beams of light radiating from His eyes gradually diminished. I felt as if I had been washed in a celestial bath. I had been detoxified and cleansed on the inside.

Tunnels of Spiritual Energy

Opening the Book of Mysteries, He began to describe to me the things that lay ahead on our journey of revelation. "As we walk together," He explained, "we will come to the place of the marking of times and seasons, and the release of eternal strategies. At these points of intersection between time and eternity, there are 'pathways of transition' from eons to eons. These are the paths that connect the material to the spiritual realm. These are the gateways into My presence. (See Genesis 28:17.) These are the places, like Jacob discovered, where ladders or tunnels of spiritual energy access and connect the heavenly to the earthly, where the angels descend and ascend. (See verse 12.) They are places of divine encounter in the physical world. There are even some specific geographical locations where the heavens are opened, and access into My presence and into the heavenlies has been established. (See Luke 3:21; Acts 10:10–11.)

"There are others who have experienced this relationship between the natural and the spiritual worlds. Enoch was one of them. He knew how to enter the spiritual realm. He was able to enter the heavenlies with Me as we walked together. Paul encountered this reality on his way to Damascus. (See Acts 9:1–8.) My beloved apostle, John, was also able to access a spiritual

You can enter the heavenlies as you walk with God.

135

doorway of transition into My presence while he was on the Isle of Patmos. (See Revelation 1:10–20.)

"You must understand that the spiritual realm is as real as the physical realm. The physical is subject to the spiritual! (See Hebrews 8:1–6; 9:23.) All life and substance are subject to the spiritual realm, and under its influence and authority."

As I listened to the Lord describe the relationship between time and eternity, the natural and the spiritual, my human knowledge and education provided no insight. The idea that there were actually spiritual doorways into God's presence was mystifying. No law of physics or science could explain this, but their existence was clearly revealed as the Lord spoke.

The Three Heavens

Responding to my confused expression, He continued to describe the nature of the heavenly realm.

"There is a first heaven, a second heaven, and a third heaven." He explained. "The human mind has sought to understand this from a cosmological approach.[1] People have failed to see that these are dimensions of the spiritual realm.

"The third heaven is the place of My constant presence. It is where I dwell. It is a place of eternal existence, and the source of the River of Life. (See Revelation 22:1.) This is where My throne is established, and where My cherubim and seraphim stand watch and continually praise and worship Me.

"The second heaven is the anteroom or spiritual realm through which the angels must pass to enter the first heaven. (See Daniel 10:10–21.) Here is where the principalities and powers engage in combat. This is the place of angelic warfare and demonic activity. (See Ephesians 6:12.)

"The first heaven is the place of the manifestation of My kingdom in the realm of mankind. This is what can be referred to as 'heaven on earth.' This is what I meant when I said to Nicodemus, '*Unless one is born again, he cannot see the kingdom of God'* (John 3:3). It can be seen only through spiritual eyes, because it is a spiritual kingdom."

The Tabernacle and the Heavenlies

"I have given you an example of the heavenly realm," He said. "The tabernacle in the wilderness had three distinct areas. It was designed to reflect the pattern of the heavenlies. (See Hebrews 9:1–15.) The outer court is symbolic of the first heaven. This is the place where the manifestation of My presence is revealed to all My servants. I have made man in the same way. Your flesh is the outer court of the human tabernacle. I am the absolute embodiment of this. I became flesh.

"The inner court represents the second heaven. It is the anteroom and the place of transition from the earthly realm into My presence. This was the place where My priesthood functioned. For mankind, this is the realm of the soul.

"The Holy Place represents the third heaven. This is the place of My eternal dwelling. My glory resides here. The Holy Place has now become the human spirit. Man is body, soul, and spirit, and My dwelling place is within My people.

"Mankind and the tabernacle are pictures of the earthly and the heavenly realms. There are doorways of access to provide for transition from the body into the soul and spirit of man. In the tabernacle there are doorways from the outer to the inner court, and the Holy of Holies. It is the same in the heavenlies; there are pathways that connect the physical world to the heavenly realm."

Concern on His Face

Jesus pointed to the Book of Mysteries. His finger rested on the lower right side of the page, about three-fourths of the way down.

"My Son," He said, "you must see these things with the eyes of My Spirit. In the days ahead, My revelation will increase and become so real to you that you will see things that you have not imagined or perceived before.

"I am revealing these things to many of My servants who have come to seek My face. I am drawing My servants to the well of My presence because I am about to reveal heavenly strategies in order to release My church for the work ahead. I have drawn each one of them to Me, but not all have responded to My call. Some have allowed the things of the world to draw them away from Me."

I watched as the Lord closed the book. He had an expression of concern on His face. I could tell that His heart was heavy. He carried a great burden for the masses of people still held prisoner by the enemy. I sensed that His beloved people, Israel, were upon His heart, as well.

When at last He turned and smiled at Me, peace returned to my heart. His question kept repeating in my thoughts: "Do you desire Me, or truth and revelation?" He didn't say so, but I knew it was on His mind.

I found myself responding to His unspoken words. "Jesus, above all else, I desire You," I said. "But I confess that there is an unquenchable desire in me to know Your purposes and plans."

"I understand," He answered. "I have put this desire within you! I have stimulated this hunger for My revelation because I must have those who will seek Me for My end-time warfare strategies and the architectural plans for My house. I am raising up generals and master builders in this hour for the completion of My purpose. My church must be prepared before the great and terrible Day of the Lord comes."

The vision diminished, but His words continued to burn within my spirit. *What are the warfare strategies that need to be revealed?* I wondered. *And the church—unless it is built according to His plans, our labor is in vain.* (See Psalm 127:1.) *We desperately need His architectural designs for the end-time church.* I sensed that He would reveal more to me in the days to come.

Chapter Ten

The Forest of Deception

The coolness from the shade of the trees quickly dissipated the moment we stepped back into the bright afternoon sun. We made our way back along the hardened yellow clay roadway. Jesus glanced toward the great valley that was now on our left. I recalled how intrigued I had been by it the day before.

As He looked away into the far distance, He began to speak to me. "You have seen this great and beautiful valley that leads to the sea. We passed it together yesterday. I wanted to speak to you then concerning its great significance, and what is taking place there, but now we will have to return at another time. Whenever you sense the gentle nudging of My Spirit prompting you, do not delay. We must not lose important time, because it is essential that My Word be delivered to My people."

His words pricked my heart like a thousand needles as I felt His firm rebuke. I knew this was an important lesson to be learned. I had failed to recognize the gentle prompting of the Holy Spirit; I should have gone to explore the valley immediately. In the future I would have to be much more sensitive and quick to obey His leading. I did not want this to happen again, especially now that I was aware of the urgency of our mission.

Then Enoch Spoke

We continued to walk along the wide pathway together, when suddenly I had the strange sensation that another person had joined us. At first, I could not see anyone, but I could feel his presence. Then the reality of who it was exploded within me. It was Enoch![1] By some prearranged invitation, the Lord had given Him permission to join us at this stage of our journey. He had come at Jesus' bidding. He did not speak, but I could tell that Enoch was very excited about something. I was so delighted that he had come. I was so blessed by the "Enoch walks" that the Lord and I were taking together. To meet Enoch in person was more than I could have hoped for. Perhaps in the days ahead, the Lord would give us an opportunity to talk together.

The three of us quickened our pace now. Each step seemed to reinforce the deep sense of urgency that the Lord had communicated earlier. Ahead of us lay a huge, dark forest. The trees were massive, with trunks the size of the great sequoias. Their height filled the horizon, obscuring everything beyond the tree line. They grew so close together that they formed an imposing, solid wall of darkness as far as the eye could see. To enter this forest would be like stepping into a world of cold shadows and dark illusions. Visions of childhood fears and nightmares flashed through my mind. I pondered the possibility that there might even be a total absence of light inside the forest. There was no doubt that the Lord was leading us toward the dark, shadowy world that lay hidden within this foreboding place.

A cold chill swept over me as we entered the forest. It was like stepping through an invisible membrane that separated two worlds. There was a sudden and total loss of light. But amazingly, as I walked close to Jesus, there was a capsule of light that surrounded us. The three of us were enclosed in a bubble of light that emanated from the Lord. (See Matthew 4:16.)

Then Enoch spoke for the first time. "Do you see it, fellow traveler?" he asked. "This is why I am so excited! I couldn't wait for you to see that as we walk with God, we are walking in His light. We are encompassed by supernatural light. It doesn't matter how dark it is all around us; we walk in liquid light. It emanates from the Master. Jesus has always been light! No darkness can ever quench the intense light that shines forth from Him. (See John 1:5.) No evil can hide from the absolute penetration of His divine light. It is unlike any earthly light or any color in the light spectrum. A thousand mil- *When we walk in God's light, no darkness can quench it.* lion suns could not compare to it. From now on, when you walk with Him, you will be conscious of this light, and you will never need to walk in darkness again."

Of course, I thought, *Enoch would understand the light of God's presence. He must have experienced it countless times on His daily walks with God. To be without this light would be utter darkness and to be entirely lost,* I realized, trembling at the thought of being without light in the blackness of the forest.

Deception in the Forest

Enoch listened with an expression of rapt attention as Jesus began to speak to me. "My son, I had to bring you into the darkness of this place, because the path of My purpose takes you *through* the darkness. It is My presence that gives you light within the darkness. (See Psalm 18:28; 139:11–12.)

"This place is called the Forest of Deception. Many of My children have come here. Some of them have forsaken Me in this darkness, and have become lost. They were deceived, despite the fact that they are My elect and chosen ones. They thought that the source of light came from within themselves, and they believed that they could find their own way through the forest. (See Matthew 6:23.) They struck off on their own. Drawn away into their intellect, and the realm of the knowledge of good and evil, they have pursued the paths of man's ideas and philosophies and have wandered away from intimacy and closeness to Me. (See Colossians 2:1–8.) They no longer walk in My light. Like Adam and Eve, they have tasted of this same deception and have separated themselves from the light of My presence.

"Here in the Forest of Deception, many dwelling places have been fashioned by the hands of men. If you search, you may even find the first one. You call it the 'Tower to Heaven,' but I have cursed it, and I call it 'Babel.' (See Genesis 11:1–9.) You see, I had to bring confusion, and I will always confound the communication of those who are deceived, who think that they can find the way into My presence by their own efforts."

Walking on His Words

The light shining from the Lord made walking in the forest easy, but something very unusual was happening. When He spoke, I could see the letters of His words form in the air as they issued from His lips. Each word drifted delicately to the ground in front of me. His words were providing a path for me to walk upon. It reminded me of what David wrote in the Bible: *"Your word is a lamp to my feet and a light for my path"* (Ps. 119:105 NIV). His words and the light of His presence made it very easy to walk in the darkness that encompassed us. We were literally walking on His words.

The Seeds Produce Poison

Surrounded by the supernatural light emanating from Jesus, my fear disappeared. I could now see well enough to explore the woodland that enshrouded us. As my eyes searched the forest, I was astounded by the many different types of fruit hanging from the massive trees. Some were pear-shaped; others had a gourd-like appearance with green, spiny skin. All the fruits had one distinct similarity: the rind was transparent. I could see through the skin; inside each piece, there was an abundance of seeds.

"You must not consume this fruit, My son," Jesus said. "It looks delicious and appears to be safe, but the seeds produce a poison in your spirit. All manner of evil is produced when you eat from these trees. They have been planted here by a multitude of men and women and have grown into a tangled web of deception. They are the philosophies and the great ideas of mankind."

My eyes rapidly scanned the thick forest, searching for the tree of Darwinism. *Darwin's theory of evolution must be represented here in the forest,* I thought. But I could not discern which specific fruit it was. I could see the seductive fruit on the slender, hardened trees of "Feminism." An entire grove of massive trees called "Theology" was cloaked in a gray darkness. These particular trees were very large, and they appeared immovable and almost impossible to cut down. It would take ages to fell just one.

Jesus headed directly for the grove of Theology. We passed easily between the giant trees. I observed that the names of great thinkers and famous men were carved upon each of the trees. I could also see that others had passed through here before us. Many had intentionally placed flowers at the feet of these massive pillars, near the roots.

"People have actually come to worship here!" I blurted out in horror. "Some of these trees even have pathetic stone altars erected in front of them," I exclaimed in disgust.

Jesus explained, "Those who never made it beyond the Woods of Theology have built these altars. They stopped here to worship a revelation or a theological concept and never moved on.

"Thousands still come to maintain the altars," He continued. "My heart is broken for them. I have shed many tears because I long for them to move past this part of the forest. You see, My son, the greatest danger is that truth grows here in the Forest of Deception. (See 2 Corinthians 11:1–4.) There is enough truth here to deceive even the elect. (See verse 3.) This truth will destroy you if you do not realize that I am the One who reveals truth. (See Isaiah 53:9.) Only as you see truth through My Spirit will it bring life. *You must not worship the truth. You must worship Me!*" His voice was emphatic. "I am the way through deception. I am the truth that is living and active. I am the Truth-giver!

We can no longer hold on to worldly deception.

"Adam and Eve sought truth apart from Me. They sacrificed intimacy with Me for knowledge. They had to hide from Me once they chose to eat the fruit of the Tree of Knowledge. When you choose Me, there is no need to hide. Everything is transparent and open."

I could see now the great need for transparency in the body of Christ. In order to gain intimacy with God and enter into the Secret Place with Him, we can no longer afford to hide anything—whether from God or from our brothers and sisters. No longer can we strive for closeness with the Lord while we hold on to the deceptions of the world. We must seek His face, and only His face, and do so with a pure heart and unadulterated motives.

Self-Deception

We stood in the midst of the towering trees of the Forest of Deception, surrounded by the ideas of man and his philosophies. The consequence of it all cast a massive canopy of darkness over us. The intricate, pervasive network of deception around me was overwhelming. *No wonder people have been seduced here,* I realized. *Only by His light can you pass through this tangle of confusion. But how does this happen to someone?* I pondered. *There must be a reason why people are so easily deceived.*

"It is quite simple," Jesus responded, knowing my thoughts. "Whenever there is sin in your heart, you are susceptible to the dangers of deception. (See James 1:14–15.) Sin makes you vulnerable to the lies of the enemy. Hidden sin, especially pride, will quickly destroy you here in this place. Pride leads to deception and darkness. (See Proverbs 16:18; 1 John 2:16.) This is why the very elect could be lost and hopelessly confused here in the Forest of Deception, and never find their way out.

"There is a definite relationship between sin and deception. My disciple John spoke about this when he insisted that everyone must confess his sins in order to walk in the light of My presence.

This is the message we have heard from him and declare to you: God is light; in him there is no darkness at all. If we claim to have fellowship with him yet walk in the darkness, we lie and

do not live by the truth. But if we walk in the light, as he is in the light, we have fellowship with one another, and the blood of Jesus, his Son, purifies us from all sin. If we claim to be without sin, we deceive ourselves and the truth is not in us. If we confess our sins, he is faithful and just and will forgive us our sins and purify us from all unrighteousness. If we claim we have not sinned, we make him out to be a liar and his word has no place in our lives.
(I John 1:5–10 NIV)

"It is very important that when My children commit sin, they quickly confess to Me, lest they fall into deception and become lost in the darkness of the forest," Jesus emphasized.

The Lord's instruction was very precise. It is possible to get through the Forest of Deception, but it requires a pure and clean heart. The only way to walk in His light is to be transparent and carry no hidden sin or personal agenda. This can occur only when we confess our sins and receive His cleansing.

As this truth flooded into my heart, Jesus looked at me. The light from His eyes searched My entire being, just as it had the day before. Nothing could be hidden from these rays of all-knowing discernment. But this time I was not afraid. Instead, I felt deep gratitude that He loved me so much that He would search my life for any flaw or hidden thing that might keep me from Him. I wanted fellowship with Him. I never wanted to walk in deception; I wanted to walk in the Light.

I glanced behind us and noticed that the path where we had walked as we made our way through the forest now glowed with the residue of His holy presence. What appeared to be sparkling, luminescent, gold particles of dust glistened as they reflected the light from His countenance. The pathway was revealed by His abiding presence. (See Isaiah 30:21.) I would never want to traverse this place without Him. It would be totally foolish, even disastrous, to enter the Forest of Deception without the light of His constant presence and His words of truth. Just the same, it would be disastrous to be in this world without the guidance only He can provide.

A Prison without Walls

Suddenly, I was separated from the Lord and Enoch. I was lifted up in the Spirit to a great height above the earth. My view was similar to a satellite photograph of the earth from outer space. The Forest of Deception had the appearance of a massive square of timber seen from a great altitude. A narrow path of light was clearly visible leading into the forest, and a brilliant light radiated from its center. I was appalled to discover that the forest was actually a prison. There were no visible walls, but the four sides of this living prison incarcerated all who entered it. They were held captive within its darkness and deception. Although they still could choose to enter and leave at will, they had abandoned the only source of light that could lead them out. Many were hopelessly deceived.

Thousands of people were trapped in the darkness. Many were standing at the edge of the forest, peering out into the open. They were sickly and emaciated. They desperately wanted to step out of the Forest of Deception into the light, but they were unable to. They were filled with fear and believed that death awaited them if they stepped away from the protective cover of their deception.

"These are the people of the darkness," I heard the Lord say. "My love for them has never ceased. (See Romans 8:38–29.) I am raising up My end-time army to rescue them from this place. Many will be sent to declare the light of My presence. I have come to set these prisoners free. The whole world lies in darkness, but I am the Light of the World. The battle is now about to enter a new level of conflict between light and darkness. (See 2 Corinthians 10:3–6.) I am about to reveal to My spiritual army My end-time strategy for this final battle."

Back in the Forest of Deception

Now that I had seen the forest from a great height, I realized that we could go in any direction from its center. Whole new realms of revelation lay ahead of us beyond this prison of deception. But I was reluctant to choose our course; true peace would be found in letting God choose for me. I still had a longing to go back to see the Great Valley. I also knew that I could probably stay in this forest forever and still not plumb its depths. I felt perfectly safe in the knowledge that as long as Jesus was with me, I did not need to be afraid of being deceived, even here in this darkness.

"You have made the right decision," the Lord said. "We will stop here, for there is much work to do in this place. Those who are imprisoned in the darkness of deception recognize the Light, but do not always comprehend it. Many, after long exposure to the light of My presence, eventually realize the truth. Others need only a sudden revelation in order to be set free to follow Me into spiritual freedom and life.

"Paul can testify to this truth. He passed by this very place where we are now. He was finally and fully delivered from the prison of believing a lie as though it were the truth. This is the Damascus Road that leads from the deception of religion into the revelation of who I am. (See Acts 9:1–15.) This is the place where My light and love overcome great darkness. We will rest here a while."

He closed the Book of Mysteries. Enoch and I rested secure in His presence, encompassed by His light. No darkness or deception could harm us. As I closed my eyes, sleep slowly crept over my being. In that twilight between worldly consciousness and the inner journey that dreams and visions are made of, I realized that I had been drawing from the well of His presence. I was walking with Him in the Spirit. How sweet and wonderful it was to drink of the mysteries and revelation of His kingdom. To be with Jesus and walk with Him is the purpose and essence of life.

Chapter Eleven

The Living Word

Istood by the well of His presence, drawing up vessels that were full of crystal-clear water. I had retrieved so many that surrounding me now on the ground all around the well was a multitude of different containers. Each pitcher had been drawn from a different depth in the well and could be easily distinguished from the others by its size and shape. Despite the great number and assortment of vessels, I knew I had only begun to tap into the mysteries contained within the well.

As I carefully lifted another precious container of revelation from the water, the Lord spoke. "These vessels are for a time, and times. Some of them contain revelation for this time and should be immediately poured out. Others are to be kept for a later season. My Spirit will tell you when to release the message in each vessel of revelation truth. Do not worry about how you will carry all these vessels. I have instructed My messengers, and they will enable you to convey them to their appointed places." His glance drew my attention to two youthful angels standing on the other side of the well.

The Word of the Lord

The angels were sorting through the containers gathered at their feet, handling them with great care. They were preparing them to be carried to the designated places where God had commanded for them to be poured out. They were treating the vessels with extreme reverence, as if they were holy and precious. Not a single drop of truth was allowed to fall to the ground. Their movements were precise and deliberate; not one vessel was tipped or struck. Each vessel was guarded and cared for as though it contained the most precious substance in the universe. The angels kept repeating to each other, "The word of the Lord! The word of the Lord! The word of the Lord!"[1] as they moved about, positioning the vessels in a specified order.

The Lord placed His hand upon my shoulder. Then with a sweeping motion, He waved His other arm over the vessels to bless them. "This is My prophetic word from the well of My presence," He said. "It is more precious than gold or silver. It is what the martyrs were willing to die for. It is what the prophets cried out to hear, and longed to receive. It is holy even as I am holy, for in it is life and holiness; in it is power and purpose. (See Hebrews 4:12.)

"This is My word," He continued, looking directly at the angel messengers, "and I have sent My angels to watch over it and tend it. He who mishandles it and profanes it will suffer death. He who presumes to abuse or distort it will be stricken with holy wrath and destruction. I watch over My word to perform it. (See Ezekiel 12:25; Numbers 23:19.) It shall not pass away. Even though heaven and earth pass away, My word shall never be destroyed! (See Matthew 23:35.)

"You must respect My word," He warned. "It is holy even as the ark of My covenant is holy. Woe to those who have refused to let Me speak and have limited My communication to printed words on a scroll. My word is alive and cannot be fully contained in a book. (See John 21:25.) Some have sought to silence My voice and hinder the continuing flow from My well of revelation. This is the spirit of antichrist that would silence My voice. It is the same evil force that has always sought to stifle and destroy the utterance and the testimony of the prophets. (See I Kings 19:1–3; Revelation 2:20.) When the prophets spoke, they were drawing up revelation from the well of My presence. Their words watered the nations and peoples because they issued forth from Me."[2]

The Prophetic Scroll

Suddenly, a beautiful scroll appeared before me, suspended in midair. It was attached to two golden rods whose ends were intricately carved into the shape of acorns. Wrapped around these rods of gold was a parchment-like material. The parchment was crisp and new and contained no writing. A red ribbon was tied around the scroll, holding it closed.

"This is the prophetic scroll of revelation," Jesus said. "It is My proceeding word." (See Ezekiel 3:1–4.)

As He spoke, identical scrolls similar to the one floating in the air instantly became visible in each of the vessels surrounding the well. Each scroll could easily be seen, submerged in the crystal-clear water within the vessels.

The words of the Lord are living, powerful, pure, and precious.

What was Jesus trying to communicate? I knew that this scroll contained His word, but it was unlike the *logos* or *rhema* word. It was a different dimension of His word, which emanated from intimacy.[3] It was like the voice of God that spoke to Moses on the mountain out of the glory cloud of His holy presence.

"This is the word of My presence," He continued. "It is the *living* word. This is My voice that thunders through the patriarchs and the prophets. This is My word that came through My Son Jesus.[4] It gives life and can also destroy in judgment.

"The angels understand its holiness. That is why they guard My word carefully. You must also understand, because that which you handle is the essence of life. It has healing power. That is why My servant John wrote concerning My revelation,

I testify to everyone who hears the words of the prophecy of this book: if anyone adds to them, God shall add to him the plagues which are written in this book; and if anyone takes away from the words of the book of this prophecy, God shall take away his part from the tree of life and from the holy city, which are written in this book. (Rev. 22:18–19)

"Those who teach My word stand in greater judgment. (See James 3:1.) Those who prophesy and say it is Me when I have not spoken stand in danger of My wrath. (See Matthew 7:15; 1 John 4:1.) My word is pure and precious. My consuming fire shall destroy those who misuse it."

Healing in the Vessels

As I carefully examined the vessels by the well, I noticed that the surface of the water in each one was like glass. The water was absolutely still, without a ripple or disturbance of any kind; there was no distortion on the surface whatsoever. (See 2 Samuel 22:31.) The water was so transparent that if I had not known it was there, I would have thought that the vessels were empty.

The Lord waved His hand over all the containers a second time. Each one was instantly inscribed with what appeared to be a number. The inscriptions were in a language unknown to me. Although I could not decipher their meaning, they seemed to be some sort of identifying code that revealed the contents of each revelation. It reminded me of the bottles in a pharmacy, except that these vessels contained the word of God.

Each vessel held a mystery or truth that could heal a specific ailment or plague, or cleanse from a particular deception. Some vessels seemed to be like vitamins or a similar type of potent substance that could release spiritual growth or bring increase and well-being. (See 1 Corinthians 14:3.) Each vessel bore the inscription of God, and the angels easily understood the spiritual meaning of this heavenly language. They repositioned the pottery as they read each label.

"My son," Jesus exhorted, "never forget these vessels of revelation from the well of My presence. When it is time for them to be poured out, the angels will bring them to you. My Spirit will quicken them to your remembrance.

"Release them according to My instructions. Some are for individuals; I love all mankind so much that I have prepared My word for even the most insignificant person in man's eyes. The cry of one hurting lamb does not go unnoticed in My ears. (See Matthew 18:12.) Other vessels are for entire churches. I will do again what I have done in former days; I will send the word of My presence to specific churches. (See Revelation 1:11.) Other revelations are for kings, leaders, and nations. As the prophets of old spoke the word of My presence, so again in this age will I release the word of My presence to the leaders of the world."

The Lord pointed to a small container that was positioned at my feet. It had been freshly drawn from the well; its exterior glistened with moisture. The vessel contained the actual revelation that the Lord was giving me at this very moment. I was drinking from this spiritual revelation. All that I had just seen concerning the vessels that I had drawn up and gathered by the well of His presence was a result of drinking from this one particular vessel at my feet. The exhortation regarding the need to respect His word, and to pour it out of the various containers of revelation when He released me to do so, was especially clear.

The Spirit impressed upon me again that some of this truth and revelation was intended for multitudes of people, even entire nations. Some vessels were to be used only once, while others were to be poured out many times. They were like the widow's jar of oil; they would be continually refilled and never become empty as they were used. (See 1 Kings 17:14.)

Penetrating the Darkness

The vessel at my feet gradually disappeared, and I found myself back in the Forest of Deception where we had stopped to rest yesterday. I was just waking from a night's sleep. The Lord handed me some bread and spoke encouragingly: "Eat this, My son, for we must resume our journey. We have much to see and a great distance to travel today.

"Always remember what you have just learned here; you are always near the well of My presence. That is why, even here in this dark forest,

You are always near Him, for He will never forsake you.

you can draw fresh revelation. You can always come to My Secret Place, no matter what your surroundings or condition may be. I will never leave you or forsake you." (See Deuteronomy 31:6, 8; Joshua 1:5.)

As Jesus spoke, a rustling in the nearby trees startled me. An ominous, evil wind was blowing in the dark forest. The enemy was lurking nearby. Satan was agitating the trees, and aggravating and giving life to the multitude of deceptions that existed here in the forest. He was causing the darkness to increase, and many were succumbing to the lies that he was propagating. But I had great confidence; I knew that God had a strategy that would expose the enemy's plans.

"We must leave this place now and continue our journey," Jesus said.

Enoch and I stood up and prepared to depart, when suddenly two angels appeared out of the darkness. They had come from the well of His presence to travel with us. They would become my constant companions from now on as we walked with the Lord.

We set out toward the far side of the forest, directly opposite where we had entered it. A soft light was penetrating the edge of the tree line ahead of us. Like shafts of sunlight, it filtered through the massive trees of the Forest of Deception and cast golden beams of misty light into the darkness. The light provided the clue that revealed our destination. It dawned upon me that Jesus was leading us toward the church.

From my celestial viewpoint of the Forest of Deception earlier in our journey, I had noticed just beyond this side of the forest a huge, open expanse of glory and brilliance. My first impression was that it might be heaven. Now I realized that this was the location of God's glorious church. The light from the church was filtering into the edge of the forest.

(See Matthew 5:14.) It was powerful enough to penetrate the wall of darkness that the enemy had established here.

Where the Saints Have Trod

As we approached the edge of the forest, footpaths appeared that led through the trees; they were everywhere. The saints who had come from the church to pray and intercede had worn these pathways into the forest's perimeter. There were indentations in the dust around many of the trees of deception; the tears of those who had knelt to pray had left small pockmarks in the earth.

Thousands of believers have come here to pray in order to overcome and dispel this deception, I thought in reverence. *These brave spiritual soldiers have paid a huge price to advance God's kingdom. Their great groaning and travail in prayer has opened up a pathway for the light of God's truth to break forth in this awful darkness.* (See Romans 8:26.)

The Lord glanced at the foot of the trees as we passed by. His behavior clearly revealed that this place was sacred. Tears glistened in His eyes as He recalled the price that each individual intercessor had paid to come here in obedience to His call. His heart was filled with total love and compassion for those who had given the ultimate sacrifice for Him.

"These are my warrior intercessors," He said, breaking the silence, for there had been a holy hush, and no one had dared to speak until now. Even the angels, gliding quietly just above the ground, hardly moved. Enoch's head was bowed, and tears dropped from his chin to mingle in the dust with those of the intercessors. This was a holy place, indeed!

I could imagine the great army of intercessors that had dared to enter the forest. No doubt many of them came with great fear and trembling. They had the courage to bow before these massive trees of deception, and pray for years and years until a breakthrough was achieved. Some of them labored for an entire lifetime just to make a single blow with an ax head upon one tree. Thankfully, others came to follow in their footsteps; they struck another blow in the same place.

Some of the trees were hardly chopped, but others were cut halfway through or more. There were even some trees that were about to topple. As we approached the edge of the forest, huge timbers had been felled and lay rotting on the forest floor. The closer we got to the edge of the Forest of Deception, the brighter the light shone from the church beyond it.

When They Prayed, Fire Was Released

This must be part of the Lord's strategy, I concluded. *He is calling many more intercessors and warriors into the Forest of Deception. He is recruiting a great army of prayer warriors; God is personally summoning each one to the battle. His request has gone out across the church.* I could almost hear the Spirit calling the church to pray.

Just beyond the edge of the forest, long lines of intercessors stretched as far as the horizon. The lines were endless. As far as the eye could see, children, aged men and women, youth, and young adults, from every color, tribe, and tongue, were making their way toward us. It was one massive army of intercessors, and they were all headed into the Forest of Deception. Surely no darkness could withstand this powerful invasion of prayer warriors.

God is recruiting a great army of prayer warriors.

The sound of the soldiers singing as they marched forward was like the magnificent harmony of a thousand choirs. Their songs of praise and worship thundered across the landscape like a tidal wave of reverberating power. As they declared the awesome greatness of the Mighty One, the heavens became a cathedral, and their intonations ascended upward, producing a cloud of glory above them.

Some of the intercessors were speaking in tongues, their faces aglow with the glory of God's presence and power. A few carried maps signed by the Holy Spirit. There was a distinct look of purpose and destiny upon their faces, and an inner spiritual compass directed them. Each one had been given a specific commission from the Lord and was assigned to a precise location in the forest. Absolute determination emanated from their eyes. They had gathered a group of prayer warriors around them to agree together for God's will to be done. Nothing could dissuade them or alter their course. They seemed almost possessed with a holy resolve. They were determined to take up their positions and pray, battle, war, and intercede until victory came or until others were sent to relieve them. They were soldiers of rank and authority; when they prayed, fire was released from heaven. (See Revelation 8:1–5.)

Through His Eyes

The last remaining shadows of the forest now lay behind us. As far as I could see ahead, the land was open and clear. There were very few trees, and I could easily see that all the roads leading into the forest originated far in the unknown distance. The Lord quickened His pace, and we headed for the horizon. The intense emotion of the journey had drained my energy, and tiredness began to overtake me. I had no concept of how far we had traveled. The Lord, sensing my weariness, slowed His pace and led us from the roadway onto the bordering grass. "Son, I am going to show you My church soon. We must traverse much ground to get there, so we will stop here for today."

Enoch was already stretching out upon the grass to rest. We had stopped adjacent to one of the roads just beyond the edge of the forest. I sat watching intently as the soldiers of prayer walked by us. When they passed us, their appearance changed. They were instantly aware that Jesus was here. They knew that they were in His presence. Many of them began to cry, and some had a golden glow of peace, joy, and glory on their faces. Their steps seemed lighter as they moved on. They were more determined than ever to accomplish His will.

Anticipation filled my heart as I pondered what tomorrow might reveal. *I am so excited with the prospect of seeing the church,* I thought. *I think I know what the church looks like, but I may be in for a big surprise. What if the Lord shows me His bride as He sees her? I wonder what the bride looks like through His eyes,* I pondered. *I really have no idea what lies ahead.*

It was good to be here in this place, where the church begins and the Forest of Deception ends. A gentle summer breeze blew across the plain, providing warmth, like the morning sunshine. The air was sweet, not musty and stale like the forest. I was still not hungry; the bread that Jesus had given me in the forest had sustained me beyond what any normal food could do. (See I Kings 19:5–8.)

I sat watching as the army passed by. I had such a desire to encourage them. "How precious they are!" I said, feeling genuine love for each one of them. I began to pray for some of them individually. I was especially drawn to those who carried great burdens of prayer. Their traveling companions held up the arms of those who carried the heaviest burdens. I felt such compassion for them that at times I found myself loudly shouting words of encouragement and blessing.

I was overwhelmed with the thought that there were similar soldiers of Christ who had faithfully prayed for me in the past. Some of them had already gone to their eternal reward. It was because of them that my blinded eyes were opened to the truth of God's love and mercy. "O God," I prayed, "thank You for the precious saints who have interceded for me in the past, and for the intercessors who are called to pray for me now. Thank You for all whom You have enlisted into Your prayer army to advance Your kingdom on earth. They are paying a great price with their tears so that the world might come to You." (See Acts 20:31; 2 Corinthians 2:4.)

The Test

Jesus looked at the book He was carrying and seemed to be pondering its contents. Enoch had fallen asleep beside me. I was very content to be in this holy place. The Lord placed the book on the ground just beyond my reach, leaving it open to the page that identified where we were in our journey.

I was tempted to look at the book, but I would not dare to do it. To look at the book by my own initiative would be to pollute and distort its words. Only the Lord had the authority to unlock its meaning. He had already warned me that revelation can destroy as well as instruct and release life.

In an instant I realized that this was a test. The Lord was examining me to see if I would usurp His place and authority. I knew that I should not seek to acquire revelation by my own initiative. That would only lead to the worst kind of deception and delusion. The end of it would be horrible, worse than I could imagine. It would be a serious transgression.

God will reveal to you all that you need to know. Trust Him!

A great calm and patience filled my heart. I would trust Him to reveal to me what He wanted me to know at the appropriate time. I was content not to look at the book. As far as I was concerned, it could lay open before me forever, and I would never presume to approach it, touch it, or even peek at it. This was far too dangerous. The authority of the Book of Mysteries is His, and His alone. *I am willing to wait an eternity before ever trying to seek Your revelation by my own initiative*, I sighed, in relief. *I have complete trust in You, Lord. My times and seasons are in Your hands.*

Enoch and I were left alone now to rest. The book remained open where Jesus had placed it on the ground next to us. He had gone to tend to other things and would no doubt return later.

A Holy Encounter

As I ascended the well of His presence, I realized that I had experienced a divine encounter with the Lord. During this time, the anointing was so powerful that my head was bowed in reverence. His holy presence was overwhelming as He spoke of the significance of His Word and the purpose for the scrolls of prophetic revelation. It was difficult for me to keep writing in my journal because of the tears that flowed down my cheeks as He showed me the saints whom He has called to pray.

"Tomorrow when we resume our journey, we will see more of the church!" I whispered in exhaustion. I drifted into a restful sleep as God's army of intercessors continued to pass by, heading toward the forest in unbroken columns.

Chapter Twelve

The Book of Remembrance

I struggled to open my eyes from the soundness of a deep, peaceful sleep. The first thing that I saw were two angels hovering nearby, suspended several feet above the ground. My memory gradually returned, and I realized that the angels had kept watch while Enoch and I slept through the night. We were still where the Lord had left us the previous evening. Enoch was just waking from the night's rest, too. Day was dawning, and the two angels were discussing something in guarded, secretive tones.

Both angels drew near and spread their massive white wings over us. We were covered by and enclosed within their powerful, celestial pinions. Shielded within this angelic cathedral, I felt transported into a spiritual realm of existence that superseded the restraints of the flesh. One of the angels took something from beneath his robe and handed it to me. It appeared to be some sort of instrument for writing, but it was unlike anything that I had ever seen before. It was made of polished, glistening gold and measured approximately a foot in length. It had the shape of a hollow cylindrical tube that was open at both ends. Simply holding it in my hand created a sensation of inspiration, and the heaviness of the gold metal made me think of the weight of God's awesome glory.

"The things you are about to see and hear you must write and record," the angel said. "These spiritual words must be written so that when you return from this journey, you will be able to declare the revelation." (See Jeremiah 30:1–2; Habakkuk 2:2.)

I expected to be given some sort of paper or parchment to write upon, but nothing was forthcoming. Seeing my confusion, the angel spoke again, "This writing instrument is also a scroll. As you write with this golden pen, the words will be recorded upon the inside of its cylindrical surface."

Walking upon Time

I felt refreshed by the night's rest, and I was eager to explore the church that lay ahead on the horizon, but I knew that Enoch and I could not move from this spot unless the Lord released us to go. The angels appeared to be waiting for some sort of signal. Finally, they lowered their arched wings and moved toward the road, beckoning us to follow them. They did not speak, but I knew that we had been issued the Lord's approval to proceed. "Show me Your church, Lord," I prayed. "Let me see Your bride as You see her."

We set off in the same direction we were traveling yesterday, away from the Forest of Deception, heading toward the brilliant horizon. Even though this was the same road we had walked on yesterday, something had transformed it during the night. There were no intercessors on it now, and it had a remarkable, supernatural quality about it that enabled us to travel through history as we traversed it. The road was like a life-sized timeline, with the years and centuries serving as mile markers. We were actually walking through time, and the events of the preceding centuries were chronicled as we progressed. It took mere minutes to cover years as we walked. We were traveling through history from the present day to the birth of the church!

The Lord suddenly appeared on the road just ahead of us. He was carrying a very old, beautifully bound book. The leather spine had a shiny patina, and the cloth edges were worn and frayed from use. As soon as we reached Him, He immediately began to speak. "You cannot limit My church to the present time you are living in," He said, with a sparkle of eternity in His eye. "You must view it through the years and centuries since I began to build it." Then He said, "There is no time in Me. A single day can be a thousand years long." (See Psalm 90:4; 2 Peter 3:8.)

The church is not limited to the present time.

The Book of Remembrance

Jesus lifted the unusual book and lovingly opened it in His hands. *What must the library of heaven be like?* I wondered in amazement. *Every word of man would be recorded there. All of history, earthly and celestial, would be contained on its shelves. I can't even comprehend the categories and subjects it must include. One could spend an eternity exploring its riches. And this book—it must be very special,* I reasoned. Straining to view the open volume in Jesus' hands, I could clearly see a column of names filling the page.

"In this book is the name of every individual who is part of My church," Jesus said. His very words evoked a depth of love beyond human understanding. "Yes, I have called them My bride, My flock, My vine, and My army, but here—here in this book I call them My jewels." He pointed to several names in the book. His finger touched the pages with such reverence, and tears formed in His eyes. "Oh, here is My church. Here is My body. They are all here in the Book of Remembrance." (See Malachi 3:16–18.) He expressed such overwhelming love for His people that I was overcome by His uninhibited affection. He knew each name; He knew every individual. The pages of the book were worn because He had turned them so many times.

He drew His finger down the page and stopped when He came to my name. Instantaneously, I felt as though a thousand volts of electricity passed through me. The page was soiled with His tears of intercession. "I have prayed for you, My son, just as I have prayed for everyone whose name is in the Book of Remembrance," (See Hebrews 7:25; 1 John 2:1.) He said, turning to move toward the horizon.

We walked side by side, and after a short while, when I glanced back, I could no longer see the forest. As we traveled upon the road of time, I watched as the Lord scanned the Book of Remembrance. The name of each saint was recorded in it. I noticed that the capital letter *M* was written beside some of the names. "These are the martyrs," Jesus explained, with a nod of empathy. "They have paid the ultimate price by giving their lives for Me. Great is their reward." (See Revelation 6:9–11.)

Many names were entered in some sections of the book, but there were other places where only a few were recorded. "These are the years of great darkness upon the earth," He said. "They were dark ages, filled with suspicion and terror. Fear plagued the nations, and many drew back from Me. Only the very brave survived the persecution; many died for their faith."

He continued, "My son, you must never look at My church again as a building, institution, or organization. It is not a concept or a theology; it is flesh and blood—My flesh and blood! My church is built with living stones. It is comprised of people. They are the precious jewels that I have redeemed. This is why I said, *'Inasmuch as you did it to one of the least of these My brethren, you did it to Me'* (Matt. 25:40 NKJV). You cannot touch My church without touching Me.

"I want you to tell My people to stop attacking and devouring one another. (See Galatians 5:15.) They are rending and tearing My flesh. I have come to put a stop to this spiritual cannibalism."

The shock of His words jolted me. My hands trembled as I took the golden pen and recorded this mandate from the Lord. Clearly, the Lord has seen how His church is divided from within, and He is not pleased. He longs for us to love one another as He has commanded us. (See John 13:34.)

Jesus grasped a large number of pages in the Book of Remembrance, flipping them over all at once. He pointed to the now totally blank, pure white pages near the end of the volume. "These are the pages yet to be completed," He said, and even as He spoke, I could see names appearing upon the pages. The angels were rejoicing as they watched, celebrating the appearance of each new name in the book. (See Luke 15:7.) I could see the titles of entire nations and whole continents written as a heading at the top of some of the pages as He turned them. The names of individuals from each country were appearing beneath the headings. The nations of Latin America were being filled faster than I could read.

We stopped abruptly in the middle of the road. The stillness provided an opportunity for me to notice that, beside each name in the Book of Remembrance, the initials of those who had prayed for, witnessed to, or harvested that person into the Lord's kingdom appeared. The Lord had recorded every prayer and each laborer's name beside the redeemed individual. Some planted, some watered, but God brought the increase. (See I Corinthians 3:5–9.)

Many unnumbered pages were still blank. Obviously, there were many more names still to be added to the book. "The greatest harvest is yet to come," I heard the Lord say. "That is why I have brought you here. You must tell My church that the time for the greatest harvest is at hand. It is now here! The whole earth is in the throes of judgment and deliverance. I am calling in the harvest. You must tell My laborers that now is the time!" (See Matthew 9:37–38.)

Fire in His Hand

I took the golden pen and carefully recorded these instructions. The moment I began to write Jesus' words, we were taken up into the heavenlies in the Spirit. I could see the Lord suspended in outer space above the earth. The Lord suddenly turned toward the earth. His hand contained a ball of red-hot fire, the fire of His Holy Spirit. Golden tongues of flame leaped from its glowing surface. He hurled it forth toward the earth with great power, and it struck the laborers whom He was calling into the harvest. (See Acts 2:3–4.) The force and power of it shook me. "I am empowering My workers for the end-time harvest!" He shouted. (See Hebrews 1:7.)

The Lord is setting His church ablaze for the harvest.

He took fire in His hand and cast it forth a second time. As He swung His arm, tongues of fire went forth, separating into thousands of pieces. He threw this blazing fire in every direction. As it hit the earth, the people it struck were set ablaze with explosive power to be His witnesses. (See Acts 1:8.)

"This is My revival fire," He shouted. "Some of the fire has already manifested, by My divine purpose, in specific places that I have chosen. But soon My fire will cover the entire earth. No nation, tribe, tongue, or people will be untouched by My blazing ones. I am filling My church with the fire of My Spirit. The great harvest will soon be gathered in!"

In the Spirit I could see North America with blazes of fire bursting forth from only a few cities. Then, suddenly, the entire East Coast was glowing brilliant red and golden yellow. My vision was expanded, and I could see South America ablaze in red fire.

The Lord said, "I am about to blow upon the fire of revival that I have ignited. It has started as a spark, but now it will cover the earth. I am releasing My laborers into the harvest."

I could feel the passion of the Holy Spirit compelling me to pray into where the fires were burning. *I must pray,* I thought. *This is of the utmost urgency. I must call others to prayer.*

"Write this!" the Lord said firmly. "Tell My servants that they must pray *now.* Their prayers will fan the fire of My revival. Warn them not to stop praying. The war has just begun. The victory can be won, but the battle will be fought on their knees in the place of prayer. They must not stop praying. It is not enough to pray for just one hour. They must labor in prayer through the night hours. They must labor with Me to bring forth the purpose of the end of the age, and gather in the harvest. This is not a day of prayer, or a season of prayer; this is an *age* of prayer. Tell them that My Spirit will overtake them and overwhelm them. I am calling them to the place of intercession on behalf of the lost.

"Now is the time to push through to birth My will! (See 1 Kings 18:41–46.)[1] Like a woman in childbirth, there is great resistance. The water of My purpose has broken. This is the time of sorrows of which I spoke to you; it is the beginning of birth. (See Matthew 24:8; Romans 8:22.) Nothing can hold back My purpose if My people will travail and pray through to its birthing."

A Powerful Release of Preaching

One of the angels drew a golden arrow from his quiver and placed it on his silver bow. He took careful aim and fired it into the earth. When it struck the earth, huge waves of energy radiated out from the center of the target.

"This is the arrow of mighty anointing to preach My Word," Jesus said. "You will soon see a powerful release of preaching. (See Mark 1:14; I Corinthians 1:18–21.) Such power will be discharged that entire cities will fall prostrate as My Word is proclaimed. I will put judgment in the mouths of My prophets and My preachers. Such great conviction shall come upon people that they will weep and repent for days, unable to move from the place of conviction as they hear My Word. I will put fire in the mouths of My prophets; and even as Jonah declared my judgment, so the evangelists will be released to call the cities and nations to Me."

Houses of Hospitality

The vision ended as suddenly as it had begun. I found myself back on the roadway of history, standing next to Jesus. I was shaken by the Lord's revelation of the end-time harvest. I knew that God was moving in the earth in powerful ways. The beginning signs of revival were evident in many places, but now I could see a much bigger strategy. I had been called upon to tell the church that the harvest had come, and I knew that many still needed to hear this message.

I could not restrain myself. "This must be the end-time harvest that the Bible speaks of," I blurted out. (See Matthew 13:39; 24:14; I Pet. 4:7.) I was trembling with excitement. "This is a global gathering of souls! The fire of God has been released, and I am alive to see it!" I shouted with incredible joy.

I walked along in a spiritual daze, pondering this revelation of the fire of the Lord and the great end-time harvest. Gradually my emotions subsided, and I realized that Jesus was leading us toward what appeared to be a humble Middle Eastern home alongside the road. It was an ancient type of house made of earthen material with small wood-framed windows. Its simple, unpretentious appearance was appealing and inviting, like an inn to a road-weary, dusty traveler. *Visitors must be welcome here,* I thought. *The owners must be very congenial people. This must surely be a place of wonderful hospitality.* (See Romans 12:13; Hebrews 13:1–2; I Peter 4:9.)

As we turned from the road to enter the house, the Lord explained His reason for this destination. "I have brought you here to show you that My church is a place of gracious hospitality. All My servants can find places of sweet rest and refreshment among My people where they are always welcome. Hospitality is an attribute that I have required from all My leaders. (See I Timothy 3:2.) I intend for them to be models of hospitality. Here in My church," He said, "you will even find those who have a special anointing and ability to refresh My servants and ministers. In My church there are many houses of hospitality just like this one."

Jesus approached a table to sign some sort of guest registration booklet, and then He vanished. Evidently, we had come as far as we would travel today. Settling down in a large easy chair to rest from the day's journey, I noticed something different now about the golden pen that I carried. It was inscribed on the inside of the cylinder. What I had written in the Spirit was recorded on the inner surface of the writing instrument. Enoch looked over my shoulder in amazement.

The ministry of hospitality is vital to today's church.

I still had no hunger. The bread the Lord had given me in the Forest of Deception had been all I needed for this journey so far. I was not physically tired, either. But even though I felt no need of refreshment, this house of hospitality was a wonderful place to visit before we continued our journey. I couldn't wait to tell the church to strengthen the ministry of hospitality. I realized now that it would be greatly needed in the days of intense ministry that lie ahead for God's people.

Looking more carefully around the comfortable room, I noticed a combination lock lying on the table beside the guest book. I wondered if the Lord had to open it in order to unlock the way for the next part of our journey. At the different levels in the well of His presence, I had learned that only He could unlock the revelation and open the way of truth. Every mystery is in His hands.

Content to wait here for the Lord to unlock the way into the mysteries of His revelation that lay ahead of us, I welcomed the amenities that this gracious home provided. Here, I would learn how to receive as well as give kingdom hospitality. These lessons would serve me well in the days to come.

Enoch was seated on a large sofa positioned under one of the open windows, carefully reading an ancient scroll he had lifted from a nearby table. An intensity that mirrored his experienced walk with God now wrinkled his brow.

A gentle, late-afternoon breeze drifted through the windows from the open plain. I was left alone with my thoughts regarding the Book of Remembrance. I had always known about the Lamb's Book of Life. But now I was amazed to think of it—Jesus has another book! Malachi the prophet mentioned it:

> Then those who feared the LORD spoke to one another, and the LORD listened and heard them; so a book of remembrance was written before Him for those who fear the LORD and who meditate on His name. "They shall be Mine," says the LORD of hosts, "on the day that I make them My jewels. And I will spare them as a man spares his own son who serves him."
>
> (Mal. 3:16–17 NKJV)

How wonderful to know that He regards each of us as His treasure; we are precious gemstones in His eyes.

Chapter Thirteen

The Bride

The lock fell open in Jesus' hands, and a door instantly opened at the back of the house of hospitality. "We must go on now," He said. "Stay close to Me!" I held the golden writing instrument carefully as we passed through the doorway and stepped out into a beautiful meadow.

Brilliant spring flowers grew in abundance, and wonderfully colored butterflies flitted about, painting the air with their motions. One was especially eye-catching; its gossamer wings were a shade of translucent light blue that evoked tranquility. Songbirds flew about, filling the air with delightful music. The atmosphere was one of simplicity and beauty. Life here was vivid and peaceful.

"What is this place, Lord?" I asked with a childlike delight. He did not answer, but moved quickly on through the garden meadow. I followed after Him, yielding to the urge to skip along behind Him. We approached a fieldstone wall on the far side of the meadow, where a gate opened onto another road.

As we left the garden, it occurred to me that this place of serene beauty epitomized the effect that the anointed hospitality of the church has on those who are privileged to receive it. It is intended to refresh and revive God's servants as they labor in His church. This experience assured me that wherever I might go among the body of Christ, I would always find a place like this, where my weariness could be removed and my soul and spirit refreshed. (See Luke 10:3–42; 2 Timothy 1:16.) A youthful vigor surged through my body.

No hardship goes unrewarded in the kingdom of God.

I reflected on Jesus' words in the Scripture:

Assuredly, I say to you, there is no one who has left house or brothers or sisters or father or mother or wife or children or lands, for My sake and the gospel's, who shall not receive a hundredfold now in this time; houses and brothers and sisters and mothers and children and lands, with persecutions; and in the age to come, eternal life. But many who are first will be last, and the last first.

(Mark 10:29–31 NKJV)

God's wonderful provision for His servants far outweighs any sacrifice we make, I thought. *No hardship goes unrewarded in God's kingdom, especially persecution.*

A Ghastly Scene Unfolds

A sudden, sobering burst of wind blew across my face as we stepped through the gate onto the roadway. This road undoubtedly originated in the Forest of Deception far in the unseen distance to our right. Thankfully, Jesus turned to the left and started off with a brisk pace. We began to walk with increased determination further into the church.

I felt a compelling urgency to draw closer to Jesus' side as the Lord's pace quickened even more. "Show me Your church, Lord," I prayed silently. "Let me see her through Your eyes and Your heart."

"What I am about to show you, very few have ever really seen or understood," Jesus said, responding to my prayer. "You must remember this scene well. I will inscribe it upon your heart. You will never be able to forget what you are about to witness."

His words carried a sense of foreboding that seemed so uncharacteristic of Him. Instead of excited anticipation, I felt an almost ominous dread about what lay ahead. I was experiencing an emotional conflict; I should be feeling great joy in anticipation of seeing His church, but instead I was fearful and dismayed.

We approached a bend in the road, and when we turned toward the right, off in the distance on both sides of the road, what appeared to be large billboards came into view. The billboards were three-dimensional. They had glass fronts and were lighted inside. They looked like giant picture frames lining the road. It was obvious, even at this distance, that they were used to showcase something important. The hands of men had built them in order to display something, but I was not yet close enough to tell what was inside them.

As we approached the first billboard, a ghastly scene unfolded. The billboard contained a human leg that had been torn from its socket. The nerves and muscles were exposed, and the upper stump appeared red and raw. The leg was centered in the frame and mounted on a background of pure white. There was nothing else on the billboard except the single, grotesque leg.

On the opposite side of the road, a human mouth was enclosed in the window of the second sign. The jawbone was spread wide open, and the tongue protruded through glistening white teeth. But the flesh all around the mouth looked as though it had been torn away from a face. Blood had begun to darken on these edges. I froze in horror, unable to move, staring at the disgusting sight. The repulsive scene was so hideous that everything within me wanted to turn in revulsion and escape this place.

The Lord urged me to move on. "Do not remain here to look at these parts, or you will become incapable of seeing all that I want to show you."

Tearing my frozen gaze from the hideous sight, I reluctantly followed Jesus. We passed billboard after billboard, each one displaying a human appendage or body part. (See I Corinthians 12:12–20.) I saw an ear and then a foot. One showcase even contained a complete torso with the word *pride* written under it on a metal plate attached to the lower edge of the billboard. I observed that each of the billboards had a path leading from the road to its base. The creators and caretakers of this appalling display of appendages had placed whitewashed bricks around each sign to form a border, distinguishing it from the other signs.

In the course of a few miles, I observed every body part I could think of. Some were so embarrassing to view that I tried to cover my eyes; yet at the same time there was such a sanctity about them that they would provoke me to cry out before them, "Holy to the Lord!" (See I Corinthians 12:21–25.) The further we traveled down the road, the more Jesus began to weep. It nearly became unbearable.

Finally, we approached a line drawn across the roadway in the dust. It appeared to be some sort of finish line forged across the road so that those who passed by would know that they had completed the specified, predetermined distance. There were no more billboards beyond this line of demarcation.

My Heart Broke

The moment we stepped across the line, a piercing, agonizing cry of righteous indignation rose up from Jesus and angrily reverberated back down the road. "No more! Enough!" He shouted. "I can't take any more. (See Proverbs 6:16–19.) I can't behold any more of this in My church. I have drawn the line. Here is where it ends!"

My hand trembled as I sought to record His words of great pain and agony with the golden writing instrument.

Then the voice of the Spirit said, "This is what you have done to My church. You have defiled the purity of My bride. You have torn My beautiful bride into pieces and dismembered her. You have divided the parts of My body and put them on display. You have exalted some of the parts and scorned others. I

God's heart is broken because the church has been torn apart.

174

have watched while you ridicule that which I call holy. My heart is broken. I can bear it no longer."

As the Spirit spoke, the long-forgotten vision of the woman dressed in a white wedding dress, who had been horribly raped, reappeared to me.[1] I recalled how the angels had taken me in the Spirit to an ancient European city where I discovered the woman lying in a pool of her own blood in a darkened alley. I felt again, for the second time, great compassion for her. Unrequited anger rose up within me toward those who would do such a terrible thing.

This is what the vision must mean, I thought, in astonishment and dismay. *It makes sense now. The woman is the Lord's bride. Her innocence was brutally stolen; she was terribly violated long ago. What I have just seen, proudly displayed on these billboards along the road of the church, is the ultimate result of the rape of Jesus' bride. This is how she appears now, centuries later, horribly disfigured and torn apart piece by piece.*

I stood in the roadway, appalled by all the carnage I had just witnessed. The dismemberment of the church so sickened my heart that I wept uncontrollably. My own participation in these atrocities overwhelmed me with guilt. Finally, I felt Jesus' comforting hand press gently upon my shoulder, and the weight of grief began to subside. Gentle, soothing words of encouragement and hope flowed forth from the Spirit like a healing balm.

Foundation Builders

As I lifted my eyes from the roadway, I noticed a cloud of dust rising ahead in the distance; it was moving toward us. The Lord said, "Behold, they are coming. Even now, they are approaching. Behold, My great company of apostles and prophets. (See I Corinthians 12:28; Ephesians 4:11–16.) Some have already begun to work among the body parts to bring healing and restoration to the bride."

I had noticed footprints around some of the billboards as we passed them earlier. In certain places, someone had broken through the brick

175

borders that were erected to separate the individual billboards. The whitewashed stones had been dismantled and thrown aside. *Could this be the work of the apostles and prophets?* I wondered.

The rumble of heavy earthmoving equipment rose above the great throng of apostles and prophets who were now close enough to see them clearly. A few of them carried what looked like architectural drawings and building plans. My attention was drawn to one of these men in particular, who passed close by me. There was such experiential wisdom in his face, such purpose and authority like I had never seen before in any man in all my life. He moved as though destiny were forged within his being.

He wore an exquisite gold ring on his left hand with a brilliant bloodred ruby mounted on the band. The name *Paul* was engraved on the metal band of the ring, along with the words *Century One.* Around the circumference of the stone, etched in the gold setting, were the words *Wise Master Builder.* (See I Corinthians 3:10–17.) The stone itself bore the inscription *Built by His Blood,* etched into the rich, red surface.

Another man walked beside him. They paused for a moment to speak to each other. One of them pointed past us, down the road, at the billboards, while the other opened the drawings he was carrying and began to study them. I surmised that the man who had pointed must be a prophet. His eyes sparkled as if there were lights within them. I knew that he was seeing with the eyes of the Spirit, and had discernment that came from the Lord. These two men seemed to be bound together in their purpose. (See Ephesians 2:19–20.) They moved in almost total unison. They had an obvious love for each other, and whenever one of them spoke, there was a deep respect and honor that came from the other.

All the people now walking by us on the road were in pairs. I was not surprised to see this, since I knew that the Scriptures taught that the church was, and will always be, built upon the foundation of the apostles and prophets. Sometimes they would change partners, but this never appeared awkward because they all respected each other. At first, when I saw them from a distance, they appeared to be dressed the same, but now I could see that some of them wore suits, while others wore jeans or casual clothes. However, no one seemed out of place.

Dispersed among this great company of apostles and prophets, at various intervals, were women who carried themselves with incredible dignity and authority. (See Romans 16:3; I Corinthians 16:19.) They seemed to be more highly honored than the others, and many deferred to them. On occasion, the men would consult them because there seemed to be parts of the drawings and construction plans where these women apostles and prophets had greater knowledge and expertise.

Soon the heavy construction equipment began to rumble by us. Painted on the sides of the bulldozers and trucks in capital letters were the words *FOUNDATION LAYERS*. (See I Corinthians 3:10.) There could be no doubt that God was committed to a massive project of total renovation in His church.

The Lord began to converse with the first apostle, the one who was wearing the gold ring. As they talked, my suspicion that he was the apostle Paul was confirmed. Others were gathered around them. Among this group were some of the apostles and prophets of the early church. The conversation made it clear that they were forbidden to pass over the line that the Lord had drawn across the road. They would not be allowed to enter the place of intended work *God is committed to restoring His body, the church.* among the billboards where all the body parts were displayed, but the Lord had strategically positioned them in the road so that no one could enter the work area without passing by them.

Jesus nodded His head toward the great throng of workers waiting to proceed into the church. At His command, they began to file by us and past the council of the ancient apostles and prophets who were huddled together in the roadway. Something very unusual was happening to them as they headed toward the construction area.

Authorization to Proceed

Each worker was issued a red circular sticker, similar to a name tag. Paul and the others would place the red tag over their hearts, firmly fixing it there. Written in white letters on each red sticker was the Lord's assignment regarding the workers' specific places of labor and ministry in the church. Each prophet and apostle received clear instructions regarding what his or her duties were, and where to engage the church. Some were assigned to oversee others; they were apostolic or prophetic foremen or generals. There was no jealousy among them, though—only a great desire to see the work completed.

A sudden, prophetic wind began to blow over this great assembly of workers. A voice spoke from within the wind, as though the words were recorded within it. It kept repeating the phrase, "The call, the call, the call." In yielded response to the message, each worker knelt and affirmed, "Yes, Lord, I will pay the price!" (See Isaiah 6:8.) An impartation of great grace and anointing issued forth from the wind. When the workers finally rose to their feet, each one radiated a divine glow of destiny in his or her face.

Someone opened a large toolbox, and various tools were distributed among the workers. Some laborers were issued hard hats. Then the Lord called for what looked like a lunch wagon. It contained an abundance of food and beverages. Each worker ate his fill.

As they ate, the workers were given divine enabling from God for the work ahead. This special grace would be desperately needed for the unusual assignments the Lord was equipping them to fulfill within the church.

There was a bittersweet mixture of sadness and joy when the apostles and prophets finished their meal, said good-bye to each other, and then turned to head down the road toward their assigned places of construction.

A Soldier of Faith

Among the many servants of the Almighty who passed by me, one older man stood out in particular. His hands were calloused, and bruises marked his body. His knees were enlarged and swollen from kneeling on them. Despite his age, he walked with strength, dignity, and wisdom. The

The Bride

other workers appeared to display a special respect for him. *He must be a warrior-builder,* I thought. *He has obviously fought many battles, and has no doubt come close to death many times. But he refused to give up,* I thought, in admiration.

A single title was printed in bold letters across the front of his hard hat: "OVERCOMER." (See Revelation 12:11.) He carried something similar to a union card in his hand. The title on the card read, "The Word of My Testimony." It was filled with Scriptures and personal experiences.

I felt so unworthy to be in the presence of this great man of faith. As he passed by, the Lord reached out lovingly to touch his shoulder. I overheard Him say, "Well done, good and faithful servant. It won't be long before your work is finished!" Peace and assurance pervaded the humble man's soul.

After he passed by, I saw printed on the back of his jacket, in capital letters, the single word *FAITH*. All who followed in his footsteps could read and see this message. "What an encouragement for us to continue on in the Lord's work," I said, as he disappeared out of sight into the crowd of workers.

Jesus turned to me and said, "I have many heroes of faith just like this man. (See Hebrews 11:32–40.) They encourage all who follow them in My labor. To him who overcomes, I will give a crown of special glory." (See Revelation 2:7, 11, 17, 26; 3:5, 12, 21; 21:7.)

Called and Commissioned

My presence in the roadway did not distract these workers from their mission. It was clearly evident to me that not only did they have an overwhelming love for each other, but they were also bound together with a common vision. The driving force in their lives was the glorious revelation of His bride. They were all there for one reason: Jesus had personally met with each one of them and called them individually to His work. They knew beyond any shadow of doubt that He had commissioned them to build His church. These servants were consumed with the call of the Master. They were willing to go anywhere He might send them and do anything He might ask of them. In total abandonment, they humbly offered their lives to follow Him and serve Him.

Jesus spoke with divine admiration, saying, "I have released the apostles of My right hand and the prophets of My left hand to the work for which I have called them. In the days to come, the things that have divided My body will be rooted up and torn down. My Spirit will demolish all that separates and all that seeks to honor one above another, for all are made by My design, and all must be honored. This is the word of the Lord. It shall be done. The structures that are man-made will be shaken and will fall. (See Hebrews 12:25–29.) My true bride, My holy bride, will come forth in all her glory."

Jesus took the golden writing instrument, and placing His hand over mine, carefully scribed the thoughts of His heart. "See! My church. My bride. She is one body without seam or separation!" (See Colossians 3:15.)

He gently lifted His hand from mine, leaving the golden pen in my grasp. When He finally spoke again, His tone reflected the passion of a protective bridegroom. "From this moment on, I want you to envision My bride as whole, for I am about to undo what men have done. No longer will I allow My body to be divided into pieces or separated into parts. The final restoration and knitting together of My church is coming. I will not allow anyone or anything to separate My people any longer!"

The final restoration of the church is coming.

The Appearance of the Bride

I turned to look back down the road toward the billboards, fully expecting to see all the body parts still displayed in grotesque fashion. But my mouth fell open in utter amazement. Instead of seeing what I had anticipated, I saw a beautiful bride, adorned in glowing white garments, radiating pure light, rising up above the road, and standing, suspended in the air, in holy array. She was transparent, like a misty vapor or hologram, but her image was indisputable.

The bride's presence filled the entire road. She held in her hands an exquisite bouquet of flowers, and her face was veiled in white, transparent cloth. She was incomparably beautiful, totally innocent, and absolutely pure. Beneath her feet, the apostles and prophets were making their way down the road to their work assignments. The bride was being restored and prepared for her Bridegroom! The wedding celebration is not far away. I was seeing a vision of the glory that was yet to come to the church. The vision slowly faded, and the workers continued their labors.

The Work Has Begun

The Lord looked at me and spoke with determination and godly pride, "This is *the* time of times, and *the* season of seasons. This is the unfolding and fulfillment of My purpose from the foundation and beginning of creation. The earth will begin to see the unveiling of My true bride. That which has enshrouded her and kept her from coming forth will be removed. All that has hindered her will fall at the hands of My true end-time apostles and prophets. Their work of completion has begun!"

A great blast of trumpets pierced the heavens and penetrated to every distant part of this place called the church. It was a definite, declarative sound. All who heard it realized that something had been released in the heavenlies. Rather than a heralding trumpet for an arriving king, this brass chorus sounded more like a construction horn. It was a declaration, released by the Sovereign of the entire creation, that divided times and seasons. Like a divine, majestic, melodious exclamation point, it proclaimed the opening of the gateway into God's purpose.

A Water Bearer for the Lord

The trumpet declaration faded into an echo of praise and slowly dissipated over the army of laborers. The Lord handed me a cup of water. "Drink this!" He said.

The cup was plain and bore no markings. Its seams were soldered like those of a tin cup. The water was refreshing, but I knew its purpose was far more significant and symbolic than mere physical refreshment. The days ahead would reveal its complete meaning, but I discerned that the simplicity of the container was an invitation for me to take the place of humble servanthood and joyful anonymity. (See Luke 22:24–27.) My portion was to refresh others with the water of revelation that the Lord had given me to share. *Perhaps my assignment is to be a water bearer in the Lord's service,* I thought. I drank deeply from the cup, draining its contents. Selfish ambition dissolved in my heart with each swallow.

I lifted my eyes from the plain vessel as Jesus spoke. "What I have given you this day I will write upon your heart, My son, just as I have written upon the hearts of all My servants." He took one of the red stickers and placed it firmly over my heart. I fell to my knees in humility, unable to stand in His presence. His overwhelming compassion coursed through my body. My heart melted in His all-sufficient mercy and unfathomable love. The metal cup fell from my hand onto the roadway and came to rest at His feet.

"I am releasing My servants into the nations to restore My bride. You are one of My many end-time workers. I commission you to go and fulfill your assignment. You will root up and tear down, plant and build in the nations. But first, we must finish our journey of prophetic revelation."

"Lord," I replied, in surrendered brokenness, "You know my heart; I am content to be a water bearer in Your kingdom."

When I finally managed to stand up, a workman's tool belt was positioned around my waist, and I was now wearing a construction helmet.

Identified by the Blood

"Lord, why is it important that each of us carry this red badge of identity upon our hearts?" I asked, rubbing my fingers across the sticker's shiny surface.

He explained, "No one is worthy to labor for Me unless he has My blood applied to His heart. (See Colossians 1:19–23.) Only then is he qualified to be My servant. This is the true sign of authentic apostles and prophets, as well as all the laborers in My church. The blood of the

Lamb must be applied to the doorposts of their hearts. This is where the cleansing and the call begin.

"He who desires to follow Me must embrace the cross. He must take up his own cross and follow in My footsteps. (See Matthew 16:24–27.) There must be death to self, so that My will in all its purity can be accomplished. I will not bless any ministry that is performed in My church in the strength of the flesh. My ministry is a spiritual work and must be done by the enabling and revelation of My Holy Spirit working in and through you."

The blood of Jesus is the only credential we need.

His explanation was clear. The blood of Jesus is the only authentic credential needed; His blood qualifies every workman sent to restore the church to wholeness or gather the harvest of souls. No wonder every soldier and worker is given a red badge to distinguish him or her.

Jesus explained further, "My blood must be applied to the heart. My life is in My blood. (See Leviticus 17:11.) From now on, you must see all your brothers and sisters through My blood." (See I Corinthians 11:23–32.)

In an instant, my perspective was forever altered. I could never see others again in the same way. The only legitimate badge of authenticity I would ever need is the blood of Jesus Christ. There are two groups— those with the blood of Jesus applied to their hearts, and those whose hearts are still black with sin and who do not have His blood applied. (See Hebrews 10:19.) I could never have true fellowship with those whose hearts are not cleansed by His blood.

The Holy Spirit Is Everywhere

"We must stop for today," the Lord said. We stepped from the road into a grove of small trees just beyond the line of demarcation that had been inscribed across the road. I glanced back toward the roadway. A host of angels moved above the great throng of apostolic and prophetic workers. They flew back and forth, busily coming and going up and down the road. They were carrying provisions for the workers, and supplies for the building and construction of the church.

Many of the angels carried leather bags, like small mail pouches or purses. The bags were designed with straps that enabled the angels to carry them around their necks. These were messenger angels, and they flew above the others. They sped off in the direction from which the great cloud of apostles and prophets had originated. I assumed that they were heading toward a spiritual command center from which orders were being issued. I supposed that this must be a place of great authority, where military strategies and plans are formulated for God's armies and kept for release at the appropriate time.

The messenger angels returned, laden with instructions for the workers. Some of them carried keys that were designed to unlock mysteries or open doors of resistance to the purposes of God. The entire atmosphere along the path of construction was filled with excitement and activity. The Holy Spirit was everywhere, directing all of the work and continually overseeing all that was happening in this place called the church.

I had explored only a small part of this incredibly vast place, but I had an inner assurance that I had seen what the Lord purposed for me to see at this time. I was careful to record what He had shown me. Satisfaction filled my spirit. *This is a wonderful place to be,* I reflected. *What a privilege it is to observe the apostles and prophets laboring for the Lord.* A deep sense of appreciation and love rose up in my heart for these precious leaders.

How the Church Functions

I continued to watch from the grove of trees, as thousands of workers joined the apostles and prophets to minister under their supervision and direction. Multitudes of workmen were beginning to pull down the disgraceful billboards and tear up the white brick borders that separated them. With great tenderness and care, the laborers were bringing all the body parts back together.

Some workers were praying and weeping profusely at the places where the joints of the body had been torn and dismembered. They were intercessors; they were lubricating the joints with their tears. They oiled each member with prayer so that they could begin to work together smoothly again, without pain or friction. The body was being restored bone-to-bone and joint-to-joint. (See Ephesians 4:16; Colossians 2:19.) Cries of repentance and expressions of genuine forgiveness filled the air as healing began to restore the ligaments to the body and covenant was renewed.

Pastors were tending to the workers, gathering groups of people together at numerous places for encouragement and instruction. Teachers joined the pastors and were imparting wisdom and understanding to the people so that they could accomplish more in less time.

"This is how My church functions," the Lord said. "Stay here and watch for a while, and learn how My servants cooperate with each other. Every person has a gift and calling from Me. (See I Corinthians 12:11.) Pay special attention to the ministries that I have given My church in order to equip My workers. (See Romans 12:6–8; Ephesians 4:11.) Notice how they work to build and to restore." I sat carefully observing the process for a long time.

My attention eventually turned to the golden writing instrument lying at my side. There was something strikingly different about the most recent inscription. The words that Jesus had written by placing His hand over mine were inscribed inside the cylinder with liquid gold. The white-gold color of the liquid created a silver outline that contrasted from the gold cylinder itself. These words were of inestimable value, indeed!

A Half-filled Vessel

The vision of the church faded from view. I had come deeper into the well of His presence than ever before. A singular vessel sat on the top of the circular fieldstone wall that protected the well. It was only partially filled. *This vessel must be the revelation of the place through which we have just traveled,* I thought. *I was able to draw up only what the Lord had released for this time. What incredible truth still waits to be revealed?* I thought in astonishment.

I had been in His presence, journaling, for over eight hours. The two angels had stood guard beside me this entire time. They were careful to turn away every possible distraction or interruption that might have drawn me away from the Secret Place. They were assigned to guard the gate of revelation and intimacy with the Lord.

I closed my journal and set my pen aside.

Chapter Fourteen

The Throne Room

The grove of trees where I was sitting began to detach from the rest of the ground, and the entire plot of earth, about one hundred square feet, was lifted up above the surface and slowly began to revolve. Suddenly it dawned upon me that I was being positioned on a terrestrial launching pad for the next phase of our journey. I braced myself in anticipation.

The War Room of Heaven

A great flash of brilliant light surrounded me, and instantly I was standing in an amphitheater that appeared to be used as a council chamber. Several rows of benches were positioned in a semicircular fashion around a raised platform. Many of the seats in the room were engraved with the names of patriarchs, prophets, or saints mentioned in the Scriptures. The seats of Abraham, Isaac, and Jacob were located in the front row. Moses' and Joshua's seats were side-by-side. I sensed that the church would be greatly encouraged to see the heroes of faith joined together in this holy place.

A single, commanding podium was placed in the center of the dais. As I approached it, I immediately felt the weight of God's holy presence,

Believers need to understand the Lord's battle plans.

even though I could not see Him. Lying before me on the podium was a large book, approximately one yard in height. Each side was about two feet wide. The book was bound with a rich, deep-green cloth, and it had been left open. In wide-eyed amazement, I discovered that the book contained God's battle plans and strategies for spiritual warfare. (See 2 Chronicles 20:15; Psalm 24:8.)

A line divided each page into two columns. The heading on the left side read, "Angelic Commands." The heading in the right column read, "Army of the Saints." This great book contained commands for the two great armies of God, and the strategies recorded in this book obviously involved the coordination of these two mighty forces—both the angels and the army of believers. I immediately sensed the vital importance of understanding the Lord's battle plan for engaging the enemy.

The military divisions of the heavenly army were distinctly marked on the angelic side of each page. Some of the angels held very high positions in the celestial army and were clearly identified as archangels. There were thousands and thousands of regular angelic soldiers listed in the book. On one page, detailed notations and instructions were recorded regarding the commission of the angel who came to Daniel's assistance in response to his prayers. (See Daniel 10:4–21.)

Every military campaign recorded in the Bible was carefully detailed in the book. I paused to read the section regarding David's inquiry, when he sought the Lord for divine wisdom regarding the threatening Philistine army. The precise timing and coordination of the army of Israel with the angelic hosts was critical. There was a handwritten notation in the margin next to the angelic side of the page. It simply said, "Rustling in the trees." The entry in the book perfectly matched the events recorded in the Bible. (See 2 Samuel 5:22–25.) How marvelous that God sends angels to work on our behalf when we pray!

"Never again will I engage in spiritual battle without regard for the angelic hosts," I declared. My resolute words resounded above the empty benches in the assembly room.

How important it is for us to understand the Lord's plans and strate-gies for spiritual warfare, I silently affirmed. My thoughts rapidly retraced the history of the church. Although our ultimate victory is already assured because of Calvary's cross and Jesus' resurrection, every new engagement with the spiritual forces of darkness requires careful discernment, prompt obedience, and complete cooperation with God's angelic army. We labor with unseen warriors as one mighty force to establish and confirm God's kingdom rule upon earth.

My concentration was totally absorbed in the intrigue and strategy of each battle plan. There were notations regarding the flight of Israel from Egypt and the parting of the Red Sea. (See Exodus 14:5–31.) The tactics for the siege of the city of Jericho were recorded, and the specifics of how to bring down the walls of the city were explained in detail. (See Joshua 6:1–5.)

I closed the book. Embossed on the center of the deep-green front cover, in majestic gold lettering, were the words THE KINGDOM OF GOD. The spine sparkled with the title of this comprehensive military journal. It read, "The Annals of War."

Lifting my eyes from the great volume of battle strategies, I stood behind the podium, scanning the empty amphitheater with a deep sense of spiritual patriotism. I was a subject of the kingdom of God, and I sensed that right here in this assembly hall the generals and warriors of the kingdom gathered before their Commander in Chief. This was the headquarters of God's generalship, the war room of heaven. This was the command and control center of the entire cosmos.

I bowed my head in grateful appreciation. "Thank You, God, for those who have fought the good fight and finished their course in vic-tory," I whispered. "The blood of the martyrs was not shed in vain." I was reminded of the book of Hebrews, where we are encouraged by the lives, the legacy, of the faithful. *"Therefore, since we have so great a cloud of witnesses surrounding us, let us...run with endurance the race that is set before us"* (Heb. 12:1).

The Holy Spirit drew my attention to an inconspicuous, closed door located to my left. I moved toward the unmarked door and stood before the passageway, waiting. (See Revelation 4:1.) I had the distinct impression that I was about to enter into the Lord's presence. A holy fear swept over me. (See Genesis 28:17.) *I wouldn't dare open this door,* I thought. *I could die in an instant, incinerated by God's holiness.*

An Angelic Escort

My two angel companions took up positions beside me. They were strong warrior angels with youthful, muscular figures and manly appearances. They wore swords, carefully attached to the loose-fitting loincloths that hung around their waists and fell to just above their knees. Their shirts were collarless and seamless, woven with the finest linen.

The angels knelt before the door, one on either side of me, and bowed their heads. They were honoring their Commander, the Lord of Hosts. They had been sent by the Lord to bring me here, and now their mission was accomplished.

These faithful warriors had accompanied me from the very beginning of this journey. Even when I could not see them, they were at their stations. They guarded the well of His presence and walked with me and the Lord along the road. They kept vigilance in the Forest of Deception and watched over the Word of His presence. Even while Enoch and I slept, they diligently kept guard, standing at faithful attention. (See Psalm 91:11.)

I quoted the Scripture regarding God's angels and their duties, hoping that my companions would know how appreciative I was for their ministry to me.

> *But to which of the angels has He ever said, "Sit at My right hand, until I make Thine enemies a footstool for Thy feet"? Are they not all ministering spirits, sent out to render service for the sake of those who will inherit salvation?* (Heb. 1:13–14)

I was so grateful for their complete obedience to the Master. I would never know what danger I had avoided or what harm I had been spared because of their faithfulness. I bowed my head, and the three of us waited together in hushed reverence before the doorway.

Prayers Gathered into Vessels

The door did not open; instead, it disappeared completely. I was instantly transported through the passageway and ushered into the presence of the Lord. My head remained bowed, but my eyes were open, and I was immediately transfixed by what I saw. The floor of this holy place was made of pure, totally transparent glass. (See Revelation 4:6.) Its immense thickness was easily able to support my weight. The glass surface was etched with the outlines of celestial maps. When I looked at this incredible universal atlas, I was immediately transported in the Spirit to the location that the map depicted. To look through the glass floor was to be instantly conveyed by the Spirit to where you were looking. Time or distance was no longer a constraint. Unknown planets, constellations, and galaxies appeared on this complete map of creation.

This place reminded me of the prayer journey I had taken months ago when the angels had escorted me to several different nations. Just as I could travel in the Spirit then, I was able to move about God's entire creation through this window into the cosmos, simply by looking at the floor of this incredible room.

I wondered if this was the same phenomenon that the evangelist Philip experienced just after he had baptized the Ethiopian eunuch. Scripture states,

> *When they came up out of the water, the Spirit of the Lord caught Philip away, so that the eunuch saw him no more; and he went on his way rejoicing. But Philip was found at Azotus.*
>
> (Acts 8:39–40 NKJV)

Lifting my gaze slowly from the transparent floor, I began to examine my surroundings. Lining the walls of this incredible room were shelves containing innumerable urn-like vessels of differing sizes and shapes. Each was identified with a special label. Some of the containers were imprinted with the names of individuals. Others seemed to be reserved for intended use in more specific situations. These more specialized receptacles actually bore the names of great evil sins, such as greed, lust, murder, and abortion.

My eyes were wide with incredulity at what I saw. I was surrounded by an astounding accumulation of the prayers of the saints. (See Revelation 5:8; 8:3–4.) They had all been gathered into earthen vessels and stored here in God's throne room for future use. Not one prayer had gone unheard! At the appropriate time, when the containers were full, these vessels of prayer would be poured out upon the earth. This was an incredible warehouse of catalogued prayers.

Positioned at the very front of the room, in a place of great prominence, were some extremely large clay pots standing several feet high. They contained very special prayers that held the power to release judgment or mercy on the earth.

There were heavenly beings here that I had never seen before. (See Revelation 4:6–7.) Some of them hovered in place as the others flew back and forth, moving majestically above me. Their mighty wings covered the entire room. They were continually declaring the nature and attributes of God. (See Isaiah 6:1–3; Revelation 4:8–11.) Their descriptions of the Lord provoked awe and reverence in me, inspiring me to worship.

Jesus has paid the price for all your sins.

One like the Son of Man

Then I saw One like the Son of Man, sitting on a throne. (See Revelation 4:2.) His throne was pure gold, carved with the greatest artistry and skill of the engraver. Its design was beyond description. Each intricate detail chronicled His mighty deeds from eternity to eternity. (See Psalm 45:6; Hebrews 1:8.)

His feet were bare and scarred with the nail holes of the Crucifixion. His robe was the purest white, and on His left hand was a ring of unparalleled beauty and simplicity.

His Vision Reveals His Thoughts

His eyes were an intense, captivating red, like the deepest of rubies. They were like open windows into His soul, revealing His thoughts and emotions. Their color kept changing to reflect the different moods evoked by what he saw. At this very moment, His eyes were filled with extreme compassion. The blood of the cross was clearly reflected in His gaze. Mercy poured out from His glance.

One momentary look into His eyes affirmed that He had paid the price for every sin that was ever committed or that would ever be committed! Just one glimpse of these forgiving eyes could totally cleanse the human heart from sin and remove all doubt that God is compassionate and abounding in mercy.

I felt absolutely forgiven; there was such a sense of total and complete cleansing. I knew without a doubt that He had taken away all my sin. I longed for every woman, man, and child to come and gaze upon His face. I wanted to invite the world to come and look into Jesus' eyes.

Words of supplication issued forth past the tears that coursed down my face. I pleaded as though the entire human race were listening, "Oh, can't you see that He has paid the price?" I cried out. "It is over! It truly is finished! Look into His eyes and behold His mercy and forgiveness!

"O God," I groaned, "never again will I doubt Your forgiveness and love."

His stare pierced deep into my being. I felt His cleansing blood circulating through every fiber and part of my body. Nothing was left untouched. I fell at His feet, weeping great tears of love and gratitude. "Lord, You died for me! You shed Your blood for me," I sobbed. "Your mercy and suffering were all for me! O God, thank You for Your mercy. Thank You for Your forgiveness. Thank You for loving me, Lord." I lay crumpled at His feet in a pool of tears.

Something suddenly began to transpire inside me. Courage exploded into my being. I was being delivered from the fear of man. I knew that from this moment on, I could boldly tell any person that the blood of the Lamb was totally sufficient to cleanse all their sins, no matter how evil they were (Rom. 1:16). It didn't matter anymore what they might say or think about me.

The Fear of the Lord

Then I heard the Lord say, "Look into My eyes again!"

The color of His eyes had changed to a deep shimmering blue. They reflected light like a multifaceted sapphire. The fear of the Lord was instantly quickened within me. His eyes were reflecting His judgment. Each beam of refracted light revealed His great wisdom and truth. Their deep azure color characterized complete knowledge and discernment. *He judges with absolute impartiality,* I thought. *There is no emotion in His judgment. It is just and swift.* (See John 5:30; 2 Peter 2:1.)

Earlier, when His eyes were red, I felt the overwhelming emotions of love and compassion emanating from Him. But now there was a kind of crystalline coldness in His gaze. His eyes demanded truth and justice. There was a finality and decisiveness about Him; it was ultimate, irrevocable, complete judgment. (See 2 Corinthians 5:10–11; Revelation 19:1–2.)

To look into His eyes of discernment is to realize that His judgment is inevitable. But it is reassuring to discern that His rulings are upright and just. They cannot be clouded by feelings or emotions, as our human judgments are. God's judgment has a purity and guilelessness to it that instantly resolves any question we might have about His fairness or impartiality.

I was instantly convinced that no one was qualified to judge like this One. He has the power to cast into hell, and He actually will cast into hell those who refuse His grace or deny Him. (See Matthew 10:28.) Any hope that we could possibly avoid His judgment is totally foolish. I was sobered by the finality of His decisiveness. "He requires justice, and no one can escape His courtroom," I gasped.

Mercy and Judgment

Gazing into Jesus' eyes of absolute truth, I knew for certain that a future judgment is coming for every person (Heb. 9:27). No one can avoid eternal destruction unless Jesus sees him through His eyes of compassion and mercy. Only the blood of the Lamb can appease God's righteous requirements. Mercy is able to triumph over judgment through Jesus Christ alone.

The words of King David resounded in my heart:

Mercy and truth are met together; righteousness and peace have kissed each other. Truth shall spring out of the earth; and righteousness shall look down from heaven.   (Ps. 85:10–11 KJV)

David spoke about a coming King who would sit upon His throne and rule for all eternity. At this very moment, I was standing in the heavenly throne room, before the One he prophesied about, the King of Kings and Lord of Lords. *Surely,* I thought, *mercy and truth, righteousness and peace, have kissed each other in Jesus, the Messiah.*

Call on His name, and He will surely hear you.

Judgment Is Coming

The Spirit drew my attention back toward the inscribed glass floor, and I heard the Lord say, "Take the golden pen and record what I am about to say!"

The Lord gazed at the glass floor. His eyes went to and fro, searching the earth. Their color kept changing from red to blue. "What you are observing is why I have brought you here," He said. "My eyes have searched to and fro over the whole earth to find a people who will worship Me and return to My ways.

"The fullness of time is coming, and judgment is about to be poured out upon the earth. Great groaning and deep distress will be heard, for I have shown you that I require judgment. My standard of righteousness has been declared since the beginning of time, and all men are without excuse. My heart longs to extend mercy, but justice cries out in the streets."

"How long? How long, O Lord, until You come and bring justice upon the earth?" I asked in fear and trembling. (See Revelation 6:10.)

"The earth is in labor right now," He responded. (See Romans 8:22.) "If I judged the earth in the past with a flood, and brought Sodom and Gomorrah to ashes with fire and brimstone in total destruction, will I not also rain down My wrath upon the cities of the earth whose great evil pollutes the nations today? (See Matthew 11:20–24.) Now is the time! Judgment is at hand!"

Tell Them I Will Hear

As Jesus spoke I observed, through the glass floor, places on the earth where smoke was rising up from the land. These clouds of smoke appeared to be a special kind of signal or message; they billowed forth like a great cry rising up from the inhabitants. This smoke did not signify destruction or judgment. Instead, these were the cities and places where repentance and intercession had been offered on behalf of the land. Some of these cities were actually glowing in the night darkness because the prayers of the saints were continuously being offered up to the Lord.

"But Lord, these prayers—" I said desperately. "I know that You see them and hear them and have gathered them into the vessels here in this room. Will they make a difference? Can Your judgment be averted?"

With a tone of immense gravity, He said, "It is because of these prayers that I have delayed My judgment. (See Jonah 3:5–10.) But the great evil has continued to increase!"

Then He instructed, "Write these words, My son!

If my people, which are called by my name, shall humble themselves, and pray, and seek my face, and turn from their wicked ways; then will I hear from heaven, and will forgive their sin, and will heal their land.   (2 Chron. 7:14 KJV)

Tell My people that this is their only hope of avoiding judgment."

So many Christians have heard and read these words in the Bible before, I thought. *Even if I deliver this message, it will fall upon deaf ears and cold hearts. Christians have become numb and indifferent to this truth.* (See Matthew 13:14–15; Hebrews 5:11.)

He discerned my thoughts and spoke again. "I know, My son, I know," He said with sadness. "They have heard this before, but they have not believed it and have not truly obeyed it. But I am not like men, who often lie and break the promises they make. I have extended My grace to generations and nations in the past, and I will do it again, but only if My people rise up and obey what I have called them to do. They are My great army of intercessors. Tell them, *I will hear them.*"

An Open Heaven

Jesus pointed at the glass floor to specific places on the earth where there had been enormous amounts of private and corporate prayer offered up to God. The atmosphere around these cities and regions was uniquely different. An open heaven was established over them. God had drawn a circle around them on the map to indicate that the enemy was pushed back from that location. Warring angels were commissioned to stand guard at these places, and great blessing and revelation were released into these cities and regions on the earth.

The other areas of the map remained dark, and some were grossly dark. I knew that the power of the Holy Spirit was needed in order to call the church to prayer in these locations. I was convinced that my words, even though they were written with the golden writing instrument, could not accomplish what God required. My discouragement was immediately obvious to the Lord.

Pour Out This Incense

Jesus turned to reach for one of the large, urn-shaped bowls standing in the special place of honor at the front of the throne room. It contained special holy incense that had the supernatural ability to ignite the prayers of the saints.

Jesus looked at me with intense determination and said, "Here, My son, take some of this incense and cast it, by the Spirit, upon the hearts of My people. It contains the essence of all My prayers of intercession while I was upon the earth. It is finely ground, pure incense. I have compounded it from the prayers in the wilderness of testing when I resisted Satan. My High Priestly Prayer for My disciples and the church is part of this incense. The entire night of travailing prayer in the Garden of Gethsemane is contained in its fragrance, along with the drops of tears and blood that were released there. The prayers that I prayed from the cross are the most costly ingredients; they are pure spiritual frankincense and myrrh."

The Father delights in blessing you.

It had never occurred to me that Jesus' prayers were stored up in heaven along with the prayers of all the saints. *What power this incense of pure prayer must carry,* I thought. *And now He wants to release it upon the earth. The saints will come into agreement with Jesus' prayers; surely the power of agreement will release God's mercy,* I rejoiced.

Jesus continued, "I was unable to release this holy incense in its fullness until I rose from the dead. I have sprinkled it upon the hearts of a few individuals down through the centuries, but I have saved most of it especially for now. This is the incense of My prayers. (See Matthew 14:23; Mark 1:35; Luke 6:12, for example.) It is the cry of My heart for the world.

"Take it, and pour it forth! As you sprinkle it upon the hearts of My people, I will ignite it by My Holy Spirit. I will release supernatural prayer in My house. (See Matthew 21:13.) My church will be filled with the prayers of My people; this anointed prayer will accomplish My will."

Carrying the Incense

"But Lord," I asked, "how can I carry this holy incense? I am not worthy. It is more than I can bear."

He reached into the vessel and drew some of the sacred incense out. Turning toward me, He sprinkled the fine golden particles upon me. I was instantly and completely covered with it, even though He had taken only a few grains of incense from the urn.

"I have made you the incense," He said. "Now you have become one of the vessels I have chosen. There are others whom I have also called here to be commissioned to carry this holy burden. I will disperse you and the others throughout the earth. As My Spirit anoints you, you will be used to impart this incense of prayer. It is the cry of My heart for the world and the church.[1]

"Now go! This is My strategy. Only the prayer of My heart can avert the impending judgment!"

Declare My Word

Jesus removed the ring from His left hand and lovingly placed it upon my finger. "This is the ring of sonship. I want you to walk in the assurance that you are My son. This will serve as a constant reminder that I have chosen you. (See Romans 8:16–17; Galatians 4:4–7; I Thessalonians 5:5.) It is My delight to bless you. My Father blesses you, and I bless you.

"I will send you to people and peoples, to cities, towns, and nations. Declare My Word. Publish abroad what you have written with the golden writing instrument. Above all else, pour out the holy incense of the prayers of My heart! Never forget that you are greatly loved!"

I turned to leave His presence, filled with joy and humbled by my assignment. As I walked toward the passageway and the assembly hall beyond it, one of the flying creatures handed me a pair of shoes. As I placed them on my feet, I was supernaturally shod with the message that had been imparted to me by the Lord. (See Ephesians 6:15.) Everywhere God might send me in the coming days, I knew I must deliver the mandate declared by the Lord here in this room where God's holy presence dwells. The strategies of heaven were to be declared upon the earth. I was only one of the many He had commissioned to sound the call to pray.

I did not look back. "Lord, by Your grace and power, I will declare Your words," I whispered. I knew that He had heard me. His grace would be sufficient. His love would sustain me during the lengthy journey ahead.

The throne room faded from my view, and I found myself standing outside the door, where my two guardian angels were waiting for me.

One of the angels moved in haste as he said, "We must go now, without delay!" We were sucked into a whirlwind and headed in a new destination. We would not be returning to the church right now.

I Was Different

We came out of the whirlwind next to an extraordinarily beautiful waterfall. Crystal-clear water cascaded over a broad cliff about fifteen feet above us and playfully splashed into the transparent pool at our feet. Lush green plants and vegetation surrounded us. I felt so alive and refreshed just by being in this place. I wondered where the source of this pure water was.

"This is another place of refreshing and revelation," the angel said. "This is one of the locations along the stream that flows from the great river of God's presence. If you follow this channel upstream, you will come to the well of His presence where we started our journey." The instant my angel companion mentioned the well of His presence, we were transported to it.

There was something distinctly different about me now! A transformation had taken place; I was completely covered with finely ground, golden powder. It was the holy incense that Jesus had sprinkled upon me in the throne room. The prayer of His heart had become part of me. I felt my heart blazing with the urgency of impassioned prayer! The Holy Spirit was igniting the incense from Jesus' heart; I was His living censer.

The Enigma

Would the Holy Spirit lead me back to the beautiful waterfall, where we had just been? I asked myself as I turned to leave the Secret Place. Could this pure stream of God's revelation guide me toward the Great Valley? Jesus promised me that before this journey was complete we would visit this mysterious, enigmatic location.

My curiosity had evolved into a longing to solve the puzzle of the unexplored valley. I knew intuitively that until this was accomplished, I would not be fully prepared for the task God had assigned to me.

Chapter Fifteen

The Great Valley

T he sturdy rope was carefully coiled around a circular wooden crossbeam located just above the opening into the well of His presence. This simple mechanism was used to raise and lower vessels into the depths of the well. Tightly woven with fine, sinewy fibers, the rope was seamless from end to end and could easily support any amount of weight it might be required to lift. The Lord had explained the significance of this rope to me many days ago. "It represents My Word," He had told me.

The Word Comes Alive

As I reflected on the great value and necessity of God's Word in my life, the Lord started to explain to me the importance and function of the wooden crossbeam.

"I must teach you something very important," He began. "Notice that the rope is coiled around the beam at the top of the well. The length of the rope determines the depth that can be reached in My well, but your heart is like the crossbeam!" He continued, placing His hand over my heart with a light pressure. "This crossbeam is essential; it provides a means for the rope to be unwound and then retrieved. The more of My Word that is gathered and hidden in your heart, the deeper your revela-

More of God's Word means greater intimacy with Him.

tion and intimacy with Me will be. (See Psalm 119:11; John 15:7–8.) When the Scriptures are deposited in your life as a result of diligent study and memorization, they become available to Me. I use them to draw you deeper into the well of My presence. (See 2 Timothy 2:15; 3:16–17.)

"Have you noticed that when we take our Enoch walks together, the Scriptures are more real to you?" He asked. "Haven't they become more alive to you than ever before?"

I nodded in amazement, instantly recalling how the Scriptures kept flashing into my mind during this entire spiritual journey.

"This is because the degree of intimacy we are sharing enables the Scriptures to be understood at a much greater depth of revelation," He explained. (See Psalm 119:130.) "You must continuously store the Scriptures within your heart. They are spiritual words that will enable you to enter into the well of My presence and move deeper into the mysteries and revelation that I have for you.

"The more you read and study the Bible in the days to come, the closer I will draw you to Me. Even greater revelation will flow out of our intimacy as we walk together. Communication releases intimacy!"

The Words of Intimacy

Jesus' words exploded inside me with the power of a thousand-watt light bulb. Clarity illuminated my understanding. *So simple, yet so incredibly profound,* I realized. *Without communication, there is no intimacy, and without words there can be no communication!* I thought. *In fact, God's Word is a crucial aspect of closeness with Him.* (See John 5:39; 6:63, 68.) *Genuine intimacy begins with the clear and precise articulation of thought and emotion,* I concluded. *John must have understood this truth when he penned his gospel.*

The apostle John explained it this way:

In the beginning was the Word, and the Word was with God, and the Word was God. He was in the beginning with God....And the Word became flesh, and dwelt among us, and we beheld His glory, glory as of the only begotten from the Father, full of grace and truth....No man has seen God at any time; the only begotten God, who is in the bosom of the Father, He has explained Him.
(John 1:1–2, 14, 18)

John began his message by focusing our attention on the Word of God. He clearly stated that when God wanted to disclose Himself fully, He did so by sending His Son Jesus into the world. Jesus is the Living Word. He is the Word become flesh. God is the consummate communicator, and Jesus is His message of limitless love! Intimacy with God begins with communication.

My heart burst with gratitude for God's revelation of Himself. "Thank You, Lord," I prayed. "You are the God who speaks! Your Word is alive and intimate. Thank You so much, Jesus, for revealing the Father to us." (See John 14:9.)

The Scriptures flooded my thoughts like a fountain bursting forth from deep within me. Jesus' words splashed into my consciousness. *"Heaven and earth will pass away, but My words shall not pass away"* (Matt. 24:35). Peter's words, penned long ago, bubbled up from inside: *"'BUT THE WORD OF THE LORD ABIDES FOREVER.' And this is the word which was preached to you"* (I Pet. 1:25).

With a powerful surge of limitless strength, a tidal wave of truth from beyond time and space surged over my soul. The words of John the Revelator inundated my heart:

And I saw heaven opened; and behold, a white horse, and He who sat upon it is called Faithful and True; and in righteousness He judges and wages war. And His eyes are a flame of fire, and upon His head are many diadems; and He has a name written upon Him which no one knows except Himself. And He is clothed with a robe dipped in blood; and His name is called The Word of God. (Rev. 19:11–13)

An Unbearable Vision

I lingered near the edge of the well of His presence, meditating on the life-transforming truth He was teaching me. A powerful sense of destiny, like a spiritual magnet, irresistibly drew me closer to the Secret Place. I had the distinct, unmistakable feeling that today I must keep a divine appointment. The Great Valley awaited me! I knew that I must visit this mysterious place as part of His ultimate purpose. Fear mingled with excitement as I pondered what might be obscured in the mysterious valley. Until now, it had remained an enigma.

When Jesus and I first passed by the valley, it had seemed like a beautiful place that led down to the sea. What I originally assumed to exist in this yet-to-be-explored place did not agree with the stark emotions I now felt. An insidious feeling of cold dread now spread over me like a shroud. The Great Valley was not really what it had appeared to be.

Despite the foreboding I felt, the illusory valley lured me to come and investigate. The pull was almost overwhelming. A part of me desired to explore it, but another part of me warned that it was better not to go. Torn by this emotional dichotomy, I began to pray in earnest. "Jesus, more than anything, I want to dwell in Your presence. I seek Your face, Lord. I desire to know Your heart."

Do not be afraid; the Lord will keep you.

His response shook me to the core of my being. "Today, son, we must go the way of the cross. What I am about to show you will be unbearable at times, but you must see as I see. I will gird up your loins and will carry you in My bosom. Do not be afraid. If you stumble or become overwhelmed, I will keep you."

Without further delay, we headed toward the Great Valley. The Lord glanced at the two guardian angels who accompanied us. "Stay close to us!" He instructed.

We passed the beautiful waterfall and the pool of peace and continued to follow the bubbling stream that led from the pool. It eventually intersected the road that we had walked upon weeks ago that led to the Forest of Deception. The Great Valley came into view.

The extensive valley sprawled across the distant horizon. From my left to my right, as far as I could see, it dominated the entire landscape. A great sea was barely visible beyond it, and the far-distant sky was lit with a burning, brilliant yellow glow.

Taken Captive

The Lord turned to me with a solemn expression on His face. He held in His hands a pair of wrist-irons that were linked together with an ugly black chain. The shackles looked like the ones used to secure people who were brought to colonial America on slave ships. I cringed in disbelief as He placed them on my wrists, locking them securely in place. I was manacled like a slave, my freedom taken from me by these awful chains.

Tears moistened His eyes as He secured the heavy irons. He gave no explanation, but I knew that He was doing this, not because He wanted to, but because He had to. *This must be necessary,* I consented. *It is the only way I can truly understand what He wants me to learn.*

Rebellion Ahead

We began our descent into the magnificent valley. Immediately, I realized that a transformation was taking place. The beautiful trees and flowering shrubs gradually disappeared the deeper we descended along the pathway. It wasn't long until thorns and briars surrounded us. (See Genesis 3:17–18.) I walked with great caution; I didn't want to stumble and fall into the brambles. The shackles on my hands made balancing on the rocky, narrow pathway difficult.

An old woman cloaked in a dark brown, scratchy wool robe came into view ahead of us. Her head was covered with a hood that cast dark shadows over her face. Her angular, bent frame was awkwardly positioned on a large rock beside the pathway. She was writing something in the soil at her feet with a long knurled stick. As we approached her, I immediately discerned an abiding evil emanating from her. The word *witchcraft* came to me, and the Scripture flashed through my mind,

> *For rebellion is as the sin of witchcraft, and stubbornness is as iniquity and idolatry. Because thou hast rejected the word of the Lord, he hath also rejected thee.* (I Sam. 15:23 KJV)

Vehement mocking and scorning poured forth from the evil sorceress as we passed her. Jesus, unruffled by her expletives, paid her no attention. Little did I realize that she typified the pervading spirit epitomizing the valley ahead of us. She was a tormented sentry, announcing the fact that we were entering a place of great rebellion.

We continued on, undeterred, and finally arrived at the last hilltop directly overlooking the massive valley floor. The elevated peak provided us with a perfect view of the colossal city sprawling below us, on a far-reaching, level plain bordering the sea. Up until now, the city had been completely hidden by this final hill.

They Seemed to Be Drugged

From this vantage point high above the busy metropolis, I immediately noticed several sailing ships anchored at the docks along the seashore. In the midst of the customary hustle and bustle of this huge urban port, long columns of people snaked their way toward the ships. Thousands of people were patiently waiting to board the wooden vessels. Some had already loaded their human cargo and were waiting to embark. A few had already set sail and were rapidly fading into the burning yellow horizon. No boats were visible returning toward the shore.

We left the hilltop and headed directly toward the docks of this great metropolis. I was eager to see what this was all about. Once we were closer to the port, much to my dismay, I discovered that the people waiting in line to board the ships were behaving like they were in a drugged stupor. They staggered forward, shuffling their feet listlessly. They expressed no emotions or feelings. Despite the dreadful look of torment on their faces, they were numb to their actions and totally indifferent to their surroundings.

Please Don't Go

Alongside these columns of stupefied humanity (see 2 Thessalonians 2:9–12), numbers of people, all in their right minds, were begging those in line to reconsider their fate. They kept pleading, "Please don't go! Please don't go! Oh, please don't go!"

Parents were beseeching their sons and daughters to reconsider and abandon their course. One woman clutched and held her husband's pant leg. With great, heart-wrenching sobs, knowing she was about to lose him forever, she begged him, "Please don't go! I love you! I can't bear to live without you for all eternity."

A little boy cried out, "Oh, Daddy, please turn back. Jesus loves you, Daddy! I love you, and Jesus loves you!"

A girl, about ten years old, with streams of tears coursing down her freckled cheeks, stood alone upon the beach. She stared forlornly out into the empty ocean. "He's gone," she cried. "My daddy's gone!" She was heartbroken. Great sobs of grief pulsated through her little body.

Doesn't Anyone Care?

Every imaginable type of person could be found in line. They were dressed in a multitude of different styles of clothing; they wore turbans, robes, and saris; some individuals were almost completely naked. Many women wore very expensive dresses and glittering jewelry. Rich and poor alike shuffled past us. Their fine clothing and business suits or tattered, threadbare garments made no difference. All of their faces were empty. Their senses were so dulled that they walked like the living dead. Acting like robots, they trudged forward mechanically, waiting to board the ships that would carry them on a one-way journey to the distant horizon, beyond the sea.

Jesus loves you and wants you to live eternally with Him.

One entire family stood out from the others. They were unkempt, and I could read the rebellion and disdain on their faces. They looked so hardened and mean. They were angry and spoke with foul and evil language. It was evident that their minds were filled with filth. What grieved me most was that no one seemed to care about them. No one was pleading for their rescue from the ship. Those who walked by them didn't even bother to look. Some individuals intentionally avoided them.

I looked at Jesus, and said in desperation, "Lord, doesn't anyone care about this family? Isn't there someone who will at least try to warn them? Is there any hope for them?" I pleaded.

He did not answer me!

Someone must do something, I thought. I wanted to cry out myself to warn them not to go any further. If only I could persuade them that they could be saved from the impending doom that awaited them. (See Revelation 11:15–19.) I wanted desperately to pour love and tenderness into their hardened souls.

Enormous numbers of people kept arriving from every part of the great city to stand in the queues. One thing characterized them all: there was a blank emptiness in their eyes! They seemed indifferent to their actions. They had made a choice and were deceived into thinking they could not change it. I suddenly realized that this great city represented all mankind. Its name is Civilization.

Someone Stepped out of the Line

A short distance down the line, a loud commotion startled me. A woman had just stepped away from the column and knelt in the dust, groaning. Her clothes were torn and tattered. Her sorrowful, plaintive cries rose above the noise of the crowded port. "God, save me! God, help me!" she moaned. "Forgive me for aborting my baby," she confessed with gut-wrenching agony. Her inability to forgive herself tore her apart inside. "I can't bear this guilt any longer," she pleaded. "Jesus, help me! P l e a s e...!" The word seemed to linger forever on her swollen lips, and finally subsided with a desperate gasp, "Help me."

Several people quickly gathered around her and began to pray. Suddenly, the Lord moved to her side and compassionately touched her shoulder. She looked up into His face. Her eyes were red and swollen. Rivulets of watery mascara stained her cheeks. Her long, black, matted hair clung to the tear-moistened surface of her face. "O Master," she pleaded, "can You ever forgive me?" (See Acts 2:21; Romans 10:13.)

He looked at her with unlimited compassion. The very atmosphere was filled with mercy. His words came like a healing balm to her wounded soul. "It is finished, My daughter," He whispered to her. "You are forgiven."

Instantly, her countenance changed. A peaceful joy settled over her spirit. The torment raging inside her was gone. Those who were praying with her led her away lovingly and began to bathe and cleanse her, and gave her new clothes to wear. They told her about Jesus and His great love for her. I listened, rejoicing in the realization that there were many similar groups of people standing alongside these human lines leading toward the ships. They were urgently trying to rescue people from these queues of death. This woman was just one of the victories resulting from their persistent efforts.

Houses of Light

Turning back toward the city, Jesus led me through the busy streets of Civilization. An all-pervading spiritual darkness cloaked the houses with a blanket of depression and hopelessness. Every now and then, in the midst of this gloom, certain homes emitted an unmistakably distinct light. (See Matthew 5:14–16.) They provided the only source of hope in this dark city. Those who were being rescued from the lines of death were given directions to these particular dwellings. Upon closer examination, I discovered enormous piles of chains and shackles, similar to the ones that I was wearing, heaped in front of each of these luminous residences.

We turned down an unusually narrow street deep in the heart of the city, and to my surprise the neighborhood was strangely familiar to me. "This is my street!" I shouted in astonishment. "And there—" I said, pointing in amazement, "that's my house! This is where I used to live when I was a little boy."

The sudden realization that I, too, was an inhabitant in this evil metropolis appalled me. As I stood in the shadowy, cobblestone alleyway, my memories unfolded like scenes from a movie. Vivid scenarios from my childhood and adolescent years flashed into my mind.

The faces of people who had prayed for me to be saved passed before me; they were all there. I could hear my Sunday school teachers and youth leaders storming heaven on my behalf, tenaciously beseeching God to save my soul. My teenage peers flashed into view like snapshots in a high school yearbook. As I reviewed these portraits from my past, I could clearly see in retrospect who my true friends were.

Overcome by the magnitude of their sacrifice, I succumbed to the emotions welling up from deep inside me. "These prayer warriors fought for my soul," I cried with immense gratitude.

The supernatural vision continued unabated to chronicle my past. My mother's anguished pleas for my salvation resounded in my ears. The dust-covered, cobblestone alleyway was stained with her tearful prayers, but even more her tears left lasting marks upon my soul. I was rescued long ago from the lines of death because my mother and my real friends prayed for me.

Believers are beacons of light in the midst of great darkness.

Faint tracks of footprints were visible on the street in front of my home. The evangelists and pastors who had ministered to me had left their impressions there during the struggle for my freedom. "This is the place where I stepped from death into life!" I shouted, erupting with a burst of joy.

Instantly, the shackles and chains that the Lord had placed on my wrists fell to the ground. I was free! Never again would I have to enter the lines of death. It would be absolutely foolish to go back. It suddenly dawned on me that everyone else who had been rescued from the lines could also find the exact place in this great city called Civilization where they, too, had stepped from death into life.

"Let the redeemed of the Lord say so!" I shouted down the darkened street at the top of my voice.

The Lord had deliberately led me to the place of my conversion here within Civilization. I would never forget this life-changing encounter with my past.

His mission complete, Jesus led me back to the docks. We walked together to the front of the line and stood beside the seashore in front of one of the waiting ships.

The Point of No Return

A sign erected beside the gangplank leading onto the ship contained one word: DEATH. There was no turning back once this point was passed. Right here at this spot, the destiny of each soul is eternally sealed. "This is the line of separation!" I gasped. (See Hebrews 9:27.)

Many saints were gathered at this point, pleading with those who were about to step past the sign onto the gangplank. Some individuals were just barely rescued from boarding the ships at the very last second; their lives were snatched from destruction and mercifully redeemed.

The ship's captain ran back and forth on the deck in a demonic fervor, frantically supervising the boarding process. He carried some sort of passenger list that he kept referring to as he inventoried his human cargo. Whenever someone was rescued from the line, He was furious, shouting curses and swearing profusely. The two angels accompanying us responded in an opposite manner. When someone left the line, they were jubilant, singing and dancing with unrestrained exuberance. This enraged the captain even more.

Get Behind Me, Satan!

With sudden, unexpected determination, the Lord stepped into the line and pulled me along with Him. I drew back in horrified dismay. "No, Lord. No! Not here in *this* line!" I demanded. "You must not go here, Lord!" But He was adamant.

Immediately, Peter's words flashed into my thoughts. Peter had tried to prevent the Lord from fulfilling the Father's will. The scene raced through my mind.

> *Then He warned the disciples that they should tell no one that He was the Christ. From that time Jesus Christ began to show His disciples that He must go to Jerusalem, and suffer many things from the elders and chief priests and scribes, and be killed, and be raised up on the third day. And Peter took Him aside and began to rebuke Him, saying, "God forbid it, Lord! This shall never happen to You." But He turned and said to Peter, "Get behind Me, Satan! You are a stumbling block to Me; for you are not setting your mind on God's interests, but man's."* (Matt. 16:20–23)

I unwillingly admitted that Jesus' actions were unavoidable. "Do we have to go all the way to the horizon?" I sighed, in surrender to His leadership.

A great spontaneous cry of victory rose up from the vessels of doom that were loading their human cargo. The officers and crew stared at us, shouting with sarcastic glee at the top of their voices. Amid a barrage of verbal insults, Jesus stepped onto the gangplank, surrendering Himself to the ominous vessel of death.

The Lord held me close, but a cold shudder of finality discharged through my body as I stepped across the line of death to board the ship. A flag bearing special significance to the enemy was hoisted to the highest point of the main mast, signaling the presence of the Son of Man. He had succumbed to death.

The moorings were quickly loosed and the anchor hoisted. The lowered sails flapped noisily at first and then filled with an evil wind. The ship moved away from the dock of Civilization, headed toward the burning horizon.

A strange, calming peace emanated from the Lord, comforting my troubled soul. It was as if Jesus had a secret and wanted to let me know what it was. Glancing down at Jesus' robe I discovered a key ring hanging on the sash secured to His waist. *Of course,* I remembered, *He possesses the keys of death and hell. No enemy can keep us captive,* I whispered under my breath, with a boyish grin. (See Psalm 68:18–20; Revelation 1:17–18.) Like the flickering wick of a newly trimmed oil lamp, hope ignited within me.

We were rapidly approaching the blazing horizon now. Incredible heat engulfed the ship like a gigantic furnace. The sails were consumed instantly in a ball of fire. In seconds the deck was gone; all that remained were glowing, red-hot cinders. Even the sea itself became a blistering inferno. Cast into this liquid fire, we were helplessly propelled toward a bottomless chasm of white-hot endlessness. The smell of charred flesh filled the air. Horrendous screams of pain and terror rose in torment, then faded into the fire. Every person on board the ship was consumed by the incredible blast of heat rising up out of the cavernous opening.

At the last possible moment, Jesus snatched me away from the flaming pit. We watched from above this universal holocaust of mankind, observing the dreadful finality of the horrible scene. He enclosed me securely in His arms. The angels covered their faces with their wings; they could not bear to look upon the dreadful destruction.

Jesus can set us free from death and hell.

The Lion and the Lamb

Finally, the Lord spoke. "Write this, my son! This is the lake of fire. (See Revelation 19:20; 20:10, 14–15; 21:8.) This is the prison of eternal torture. This is the place of final judgment. All those who reject Me will perish in this awful torment."

As I wrote these words with the golden writing instrument, several images were simultaneously engraved on the outside of the cylinder. The outlines of two keys appeared, expertly scrolled upon the surface. One was the key of death, and the other was the key of hell. Above the key of death, written in beautiful script, were the words *Lion of Judah.* Above the key of hell were the words *He is worthy to open the scroll.* (See Revelation 5:1–5.)

Rotating the pen in my hand, I discovered that the opposite side also bore a new icon. The figure of a lamb, raised slightly above the surface, was emblazoned upon it. The inscription read, "Lamb of God." (See John 1:29, 36.)

The instant I read the inscription, I was lifted high above the great sea and transported back toward Civilization. The intense heat from the burning chasm gradually faded, but the dreadful scene remained indelibly etched in my mind. We passed over the great metropolis and came to rest on the hilltop overlooking the city, from which we had first viewed the inhabited plain by the Sea of Death.

The Streets of Evil

I looked out again over this vast city. Thousands of avenues and streets led in every direction. Their names had a peculiar quality about them; they served to depict the character of the people who resided along them. The titles described a multitude of despicable things: Adultery, Murder, Greed, Prostitution, Drugs, Alcohol, Abortion, War, Disease, Torture, Lust, Hatred, Jealousy, Envy, Pornography, Lying, Deception, Idolatry, Witchcraft, Pride—the list was endless. These were the addresses of Civilization.

Everyone who lived in a particular neighborhood manifested the same personality and behavior. They characterized the very problems that were identified by the names of the streets on which they lived. Along these passageways, entire families, clans, and tribes indulged in the identifying sin that dominated their community. Every succeeding generation propagated the sins of its fathers. (See Exodus 20:5.) The same sins were repeated over and over again. It was humanly impossible to escape the family curse through human endeavors.

Many of the streets converged into great plazas or parks. These became common gathering places where a host of evil deeds were acted out in one continuous theatrical spectacle of lewdness and degradation.

The city was a gigantic moral sewer; every neighborhood was filled with all manner of evil.

Demonic Activity

Demonic creatures were moving back and forth above the city. They wielded great power and authority over entire regions of Civilization. Many of these demonic spirits were gathering together in clandestine groups to discuss malevolent strategies. Their intention was to establish strongholds over entire people groups among the population. Evil spirits ran rampant, moving about unrestrained. The entirety of Civilization was covered by a multitude of invisible, wicked principalities and powers in the spirit realm. (See Ephesians 6:12.)

Directly above all this demonic activity, on a higher dimension of spiritual power, glistening white angelic beings were moving back and forth. Here and there, throughout the city, shafts of brilliant white light connected this upper heaven to specific sections of the metropolis. Some of the neighborhoods had apparently waged spiritual warfare against the dominating malevolent spirits and were able to achieve an open heaven above their community. The entire scene reminded me of the incredible throne room of heaven and the smoke that rose up from places on the earth where the kingdom of God prevailed.

Great wisdom, revelation, and anointing were flooding into these locations from the presence of God. I could actually discern angels ascending and descending through these portals of access established by the prayers of the saints. Although there was great darkness throughout most of the city, it was obvious that in these reclaimed places, there was a wonderful refuge of righteousness, peace, and joy.

Human Lamps

People were fanning out into the darkness of the city from these places of celestial illumination. They possessed a spiritual light that shone brightly from within them. This inner radiance dispelled the darkness wherever they went. Possessors of divine revelation, these human torches, set ablaze by the love of God, offered the only hope of true deliverance in this immense prison of evil called Civilization.

War and unrest pervaded the metropolis. Only those who walked in the light were able to resist the besetting sins of the land; they possessed a peace and joy unknown to the rest of the population. (See Romans 14:17.) Yet their environment so grieved their spirits that they constantly prayed as they went about their daily activities.

Only One Solution

"Lord, what is this about?" I asked. "Why are You showing this to me?"

"What you see is mankind," He said. "This is the realm of all flesh, called Civilization. This is why My Spirit is so grieved. Everywhere you look, you see evil and corruption. What I originally created to be beautiful, mankind has defiled with all manner of evil. Their hearts are desperately wicked. (See Jeremiah 17:9.) That is why I brought you here. I want you to see that there is only one solution to this evil.

Our battle is against the spiritual forces of wickedness.

"Look here!" He commanded.

When I turned to look in the direction of His voice, I was shocked to see Jesus hanging upon the cross. Here on this hilltop above the vast city of Civilization, everyone living below us could clearly see Him from any location within the city.

"The place where you stand is called Calvary," He cried. "I was crucified here for all mankind. The price has been paid once and for all. Every sin ever committed throughout all the ages is paid for," He said with great compassion. (See Isaiah 53:3–12; Romans 6:10.)

"This is the message you must write: *'It is not too late! I will come and save all who repent and believe in Me.'* But time is very short. Soon, the great and terrible Day of Judgment will be released on the earth."

The undeniable scene of the Crucifixion screamed with a present reality. His love has not changed despite the passing of the centuries. His mercy is still available to the masses of mankind sprawled upon the plain of Civilization.

But will they respond today? I wondered.

I Began to Shout

The words *once for all* rose up within me like fire in my bones. I could not hold them back. I lifted my voice and began to shout with all the strength that I could summon, "Once for all! Once for all! Once for all!" I passionately cried at the top of my voice toward the great city below me, hoping to awaken some lost soul to the reality of the Savior's love. I knew that if anyone, no matter how much he was entangled in the sin of Civilization, would call upon Jesus, he would be saved from destruction. (See Acts 2:21; Romans 10:13.)

Enoch suddenly appeared beside me at the foot of the cross, looking down at Civilization. He spoke with a solemn tone in his voice. "This is what God revealed to me many thousands of years ago," he declared. "I saw the end of the age, and the return of the Son of Man to judge the earth and all who are in it.

"Now the end of the age is drawing near. The heavens will open with a declaration of eternal and cataclysmic judgment, and the Lord will return. But there is still time; He is not willing that any should perish. He wants everyone to be saved." (See 2 Peter 3:9.)

I recalled Enoch's words, recorded in the book of Jude:

And about these also Enoch, in the seventh generation from Adam, prophesied, saying, "Behold, the Lord came with many thousands of His holy ones, to execute judgment upon all, and to convict all the ungodly of all their ungodly deeds which they have done in an ungodly way, and of all the harsh things which ungodly sinners have spoken against Him." (Jude 14–15)

217

A Royal Vessel

As if I were in the concluding scene of a great epic, I was instantly transported back to the well of His presence. A tall urn stood at my feet. It was different from any of the others gathered about me. It was made of solid gold and had the royal seal of the King of Kings on the outside of it. Instead of water, it contained pure blood. I dared not touch it. There was no scroll inside it like all the others, but I quickly realized that none was needed.

This is the holiest of all the vessels, I thought. *This is the blood of the Lamb that takes away the sins of the world. Only this can suffice! Only this blood can cleanse and absolve and set mankind free. This is the blood of Jesus, the Word become flesh!*

Written upon My Heart

During this entire spiritual journey, God had used me as His scribe to record the vision and the word of His presence. But now, the words that were inscribed on the surfaces of the golden pen were becoming part of me. The Holy Spirit was supernaturally writing them upon my heart. (See Jeremiah 31:33; 2 Corinthians 3:21.) The truths were being indelibly etched in my soul. Like Ezekiel, I had become the message.

> Then He said to me, "Son of man, eat what you find; eat this scroll, and go, speak to the house of Israel." So I opened my mouth, and He fed me this scroll. And He said to me, "Son of man, feed your stomach, and fill your body with this scroll which I am giving you." Then I ate it, and it was sweet as honey in my mouth. (Ezek. 3:1–3)

Chapter Sixteen

The Commission

It is finished!" one of the angels declared to me. "But we will not leave you. What He has revealed to you must be carefully guarded. The message must now be delivered to the world. The Holy Spirit will anoint you to proclaim it. The Lord has commissioned you to write the vision and declare it! Wherever you go, we will be with you."

Tablets of Gold

The angel's announcement jogged my memory, and a forgotten dream that I had received several months ago rushed into my thoughts. Up until this moment, the dream had remained an unsolved mystery. I could not understand what the Lord was trying to say to me; but now, in light of the angel's words, it began to unravel.

In the dream, two brilliant pieces of pure gold appeared. They were large, rectangular, flat sheets of metal, approximately the size of a common blanket. They gleamed with an unalloyed luster. Both pieces appeared to be identical. I assumed, at the time, that they represented the presence and the glory of God.

One of these gold objects was supernaturally deposited within my body and disappeared from sight. The other piece was so sacred that it was unapproachable. I knew it was so holy that anyone who might mishandle it would die. I carefully hid this second piece of gold in a wooded area, beyond the sight or access of others, lest they foolishly approach it and die. (See I Chronicles 13:9–10.) In the dream, I refused to reveal its location to anyone.

When I first sought to interpret this dream, I thought that the golden object that was deposited within me might indicate that God allows only a measure of His glory to abide within us. The extent of God's glory that others detect within us is certainly less than the fullness of His own magnificence. But it is still, in essence, an authentic reflection of the awesome glory of the living God manifested within a mortal being! The difference is that it is imparted to us in a form that is humanly endurable. It will not destroy us!

Could this be likened to the glory of God that Israel saw reflected on the face of Moses? I pondered (Exod. 32:49–30, 33–35). *Could this blanket of gold be the glory of God, which covers His servants?* Perhaps this is what the dream means, I surmised. *God's glory is the same, no matter the degree to which it is manifested. His glory is always His glory! He will not share it with another.* (See Exodus 15:11; Isaiah 48:11.)

While this idea made sense, I still was not sure of the interpretation. I knew I was missing an important key that would unlock the true meaning of the dream. In an instant, the Holy Spirit gave me supernatural insight. The two pieces of gold were not blankets; they were parchments! They were supernatural tablets upon which to inscribe the vision God was giving me. I had already used the first gold parchment to record the vision revealed to me in the well of His presence. It was written with the golden pen; but the pen was also a scroll. This golden scroll was deposited within my being, much like the scrolls that appeared within each clay vessel beside the well of His presence. The revelation was written on the tablet of my heart by the hand of the Holy Spirit.

The second gold parchment is hidden away in a secret place. It is reserved for God's specific strategies regarding the final days yet to be revealed. Upon it will be written the full revelation of the hidden kingdom.

God has only disclosed the portion of His purposes and plans that we need for this season. Much of the mystery of His hidden wisdom is still concealed and can be discovered only by His divine appointment in the intimacy of His presence. (See Proverbs 25:2.) It remains out of reach, beyond our access, hidden deep within the well of His presence. It is *Much of God's wisdom is still hidden and is yet to be revealed.* sacred and unapproachable. It is beyond us. It is yet to be revealed. And in the well beneath it, there is a part of His glory that He has reserved only for Himself.

One Vessel Excelled Them All

The angels were carefully guarding all the clay vessels that had been drawn from the well of His presence. I scanned the incredible assortment of containers with intense satisfaction and joy. Each one contained a message from the Lord that waited to be delivered. I was so humbled by the opportunity and privilege of releasing their contents. I had an unshakable confidence that the Holy Spirit would impart the truth of each revelation to those who listened in faith. These were spiritual words, intended for those who had spiritual ears to hear. (See I Corinthians 2:13.)

One extraordinary vessel, the golden vessel that contained the blood of Jesus, far exceeded all the others in value. This one was priceless. It carried the most powerful substance in the entire universe. There was such authority contained in the message of His blood that nothing could overcome its ability to transform those who received it.

I pondered the formidable task ahead. "It will require more than an entire lifetime to proclaim the messages contained in all of these vessels of revelation standing before me," I admitted to the angels. "It's so humbling," I confessed. "I have plumbed only a very small part of the well's depths. There is an eternal river of His presence still available to those who will come and drink. Wisdom and revelation belong to Him!" (See Romans 11:33; Matthew 13:34–35.) I stood in awe of the unfathomable depths of God's love and mercy.

A Burning Desire

Overwhelmed by the sobering task that lay ahead of me, the words of the apostle Paul struck a chord in my heart: *"My little children, for whom I labor in birth again until Christ is formed in you"* (Gal. 4:19 NKJV). Paul was possessed by a singular motive. A burning desire filled Him with such passion that it drove him to spend every waking hour proclaiming the message of the revelation of Jesus. He longed for Christ to be formed within every person. This burden overshadowed all others. Paul's labor of love was all-consuming.

"Until Christ be formed in you! Until Christ be formed *in you!*" The Holy Spirit branded this truth into my heart with searing holy fire. It kept repeating over and over—one single message towering above the rest.

This is more than a noble thought; this is the greatest revelation ever drawn from the well of His presence, I reasoned. *All the prophets of old, from the beginning of history, have acknowledged the immensity of this towering truth. Surely, Paul spoke on their behalf when he wrote about this mystery:*

> *I was made a minister according to the stewardship from God bestowed on me for your benefit, that I might fully carry out the preaching of the word of God, that is, the mystery which has been hidden from the past ages and generations; but has now been manifested to His saints, to whom God willed to make known what is the riches of the glory of this mystery among the Gentiles, which is Christ in you, the hope of glory. And we proclaim Him, admonishing every man and teaching every man with all wisdom, that we may present every man complete in Christ. And for this purpose also I labor, striving according to His power, which mightily works within me.*
>
> (Col. 1:25–29)

I finally understood the ultimate reason why the Lord had drawn me into His presence. The same burning passion that the Lord imparted to

Paul, and thousands of others, was now burning within me. I longed to see Jesus Christ formed in every person. Every individual believer must be filled with His presence and made into His likeness. Jesus *must* fill all things. (See Ephesians 4:10.) He desires *intimacy* with all His creation!

The Apostolic Heart-Cry

Paul's prayer was the prayer of my own heart and the cry of my soul:

> *For this reason I too, having heard of the faith in the Lord Jesus which exists among you, and your love for all the saints, do not cease giving thanks for you, while making mention of you in my prayers; that the God of our Lord Jesus Christ, the Father of glory, may give to you a spirit of wisdom and of revelation in the knowledge of Him. I pray that the eyes of your heart may be enlightened, so that you may know what is the hope of His calling, what are the riches of the glory of His inheritance in the saints, and what is the surpassing greatness of His power toward us who believe. These are in accordance with the working of the strength of His might which He brought about in Christ, when He raised Him from the dead, and seated Him at His right hand in the heavenly places, far above all rule and authority and power and dominion, and every name that is named, not only in this age, but also in the one to come. And He put all things in subjection under His feet, and gave Him as head over all things to the church, which is His body, the fullness of Him who fills all in all.*
> (Eph. 1:15–23)

The Roadway of Life

The pathway from the well of His presence gradually wound its way up a slight incline toward a well-traveled road nearby. The silence and tender intimacy that I had so enjoyed by being near the well quickly faded as I made my way along the narrow path. The road ahead was busy with the hustle and bustle of everyday life. The din of its noisy traffic gradually invaded the quietness of this Secret Place.

Everyday life is trivial compared with time in the Secret Place. Peering out from behind the leafy bushes bordering the roadway, I managed to remain unnoticed by the throngs of preoccupied travelers who hurried here and there, busily engaged in the traffic and commerce of everyday life. They were so engrossed in their affairs, yet all their activities and haste seemed so trivial and insignificant.

The Secret Entrance

Reluctantly, I stepped from the sequestered path onto the hectic thoroughfare. The bushes closed behind me, and the path leading to the well of His presence became obscured. I stood in the roadway, heavy-hearted, watching all the people going about their lives as usual.

I was distressed to see that the multitudes passing by never noticed the concealed entrance to the well. I seemed to be the only one who knew where the hidden opening was located. I knew that this was the sole place of access onto the path that led to the well of His presence. I determined never to lose sight of its location myself.

Every now and then, a curious traveler would stop momentarily at the spot where I had stepped from the path onto the roadway. He or she would examine the unusual shrubbery and then quickly move on. (See Matthew 7:13–14.) Some individuals were slightly more inquisitive than others and would linger for a while to ponder the meaning of the anomaly. Easily distracted, they resumed their daily routines, forfeiting the incredible treasure just beyond the edge of the road. An exceptional few actually turned aside from their busyness on the roadway of life to disappear into the bushes. They were the determined ones! In their passionate pursuit of God, they discovered the path leading to the well of His presence. An inner compass directed them to the entrance. The Holy Spirit was drawing them into God's presence. (See Matthew 6:5–6.)

Their countenances were dramatically altered when they eventually returned to the roadway of life. An unmistakable peace radiated from their faces. I knew the reason behind their transformation! They had been drinking from the well of His presence, enjoying sweet intimacy with the Lord. They had become the people of His presence. Every one of them paid careful attention to where the entrance to the path was located. They had every intention of returning to the well. But I knew that some of them would never come back. The sacrifice would be more than they were willing to pay.

Tomorrow I Will Return

Great contentment and assurance washed over me. *The way into His presence is always available,* I thought with great delight, *not only for me, but also for everyone willing to turn aside and seek His face.* (See Hebrews 10:19–22.)

I stood transfixed in the middle of the busy avenue, studying the features of those passing by. Suddenly it dawned upon me, *I have seen these empty faces before in the Great Valley,* I shuddered.

I must tell them! I realized, as my pulse quickened with a sense of urgency. *I must tell them about the Secret Place.*

A sudden warmth filled my breast, and I felt the gentle impression of an unseen hand upon my heart. "Yes, Lord," I said, "I will pour out the vessel of truth now."

"Those who seek Him with all their heart will find Him!" I shouted, boldly announcing this powerful truth to each individual within the sound of my voice. Each new declaration strengthened my own resolve to seek Him with all my heart.

"I promise You, Lord," I vowed. "Tomorrow, I will return to walk with You again, like Enoch. I will enter the Secret Place and make my way down the path that leads to the well of Your presence. I know You will be waiting."

Notes

Part One: Dreams and Visions

Chapter One: In the Spirit I Can Fly

[1] It may be helpful to compare this experience with that of the prophet and visionary Ezekiel. The word of the Lord appeared to him in four different visions: the cherubim (Ezek. 1:1–3:13), the vision of godlessness and coming judgment (Ezek. 8:1–11:25), the burning vine (Ezek. 15), and the vision of the dry bones (Ezek. 37:1–14). On several occasions, Ezekiel was directed and instructed by the words and actions of angelic beings.

He stands as a fitting Old Testament example of being taken on a spiritual journey by God. In Ezekiel 8:3 we read,

> And He stretched out the form of a hand and caught me by a lock of my head; and the Spirit lifted me up between earth and heaven and brought me in the visions of God to Jerusalem.

In the New Testament, Phillip is another example of being transported by the Spirit for the purposes of God. In Acts 8:39–40 we read,

> And when they came up out of the water, the Spirit of the Lord snatched Phillip away; and the eunuch saw him no more, but went on his way rejoicing. But Phillip found himself at Azotus.

God has the power and ability to transport us by the Spirit in the physical realm, whenever and wherever His purposes require it.

Chapter 2: Where Is My Passport?

[1] The young boy Samuel learned to recognize the voice of God through the instruction of his spiritual mentor, Eli, the priest. See I Samuel 3.

[2] Brother Lawrence, a post-reformation monk, recorded his spiritual insights in the classic French work, *The Practice of the Presence of God.* The following quotations provide us with a glimpse into the heart and life of this famous Christian mystic.

> When outward business diverted him a little from the thought of God, a fresh remembrance coming from God invested his soul, and so inflamed and transported him that it was difficult for him to contain himself. That he was more united to God in his outward employments, than when he left them for devotion in retirement.

> That the most excellent method he had found for going to God, was that of doing our common business without any view of pleasing men and (as far as we are capable) purely for the love of God. That it was a great delusion to think that the times of prayer ought to differ from other times. That we are strictly obliged to adhere to God by action in the time of action, as by prayer in its season.

> "The time of business," said he, "does not with me differ from the time of prayer; and in the noise and clutter of my kitchen, while several persons are at the same time calling for different things, I possess God in as great tranquillity as if I were upon my knees at the Blessed Sacrament." [See Brother Lawrence, *The Practice of the Presence of God,* version I (Albany, OR: Ages Software, 1997), 11, 14, 16. Also see the reprint by Whitaker House, New Kensington, PA, 1982.]

Brother Lawrence was able to transcend the barrier between the sacred and the secular, established by the institutional religion of his day. He found God in every aspect of life. His experience reflected the tide of opinion that was slowly surfacing against the monastic and religious orders being the only viable avenue to intimacy with God.

Today, we are experiencing the opposite trend. The contemporary religious philosophical worldview maintains the idea of no separation between sacred and secular, but the grassroots heart-cry of God's people is to turn from worldliness and seek His holy presence. We have become weary of accepting the good in place of the best. The church is repenting of its unwillingness to pay the price for true intimacy with God in the Holy Place.

[3] There are several excellent books on the subject of dreams and interpretation that I highly recommend as a resource for further study on this subject:

> Herman Riffel, *Your Dreams: God's Neglected Gift* (Lincoln, VA: Chosen Books, 1981).
> Herman Riffel, *Voice of God: The Significance of Dreams, Visions, Revelations* (Wheaton, IL: Tyndale, 1978).
> John A. Sanford, *Dreams: God's Forgotten Language* (New York: J. B. Lippincott Co., 1968).

Chapter Three: The End of the Beginning

[1] Matt. 11:15; 13:9, 43; Mark 4:9, 23; 7:16; Luke 8:8; 14:35; Rev. 2:7, 11, 17, 29; 3:6, 13, 22.

[2] The word *regret* is derived from the Greek word *metamelomai,* which means "to regret or repent." It is used to refer to the emotion of mourning the absence or death of someone. It connotes deep sorrow. Regret is an expression of grief or pain tinged with the distressing emotions of disappointment, longing, or remorse. It is helpful to compare regret with *godly sorrow* that leads to repentance. (See 2 Corinthians 7:8–11.)

Chapter Four: The Footsteps of Enoch

[1] The Books of Enoch are available in print. See James H. Charlesworth. *The Old Testament Pseudepigrapha, Apocalyptic Literature, and Testaments,* vol. 1 (New York: Doubleday, 1983).

[2] The concept of the "life force" finds its origin in Creation. The foundational fact of life is that its source is God. We are alive because God breathed life into us (Gen. 2:7). Life itself is a consequence of the presence of the Spirit of God, the Life Force, and all our activities are dependent upon this life-giving, vitalizing power from God. When God sends forth His Spirit, things are created, and they live; when He withdraws His Spirit, they die (Ps. 104:29–30). It follows that the secret, and the source, of life is having a relationship with God.

The Tree of Life in the midst of the Garden of Eden provided immortality for man (Gen. 2:9; 3:22, 24). As long as Adam and Eve had free access to this tree, its fruit sustained them. When they committed sin by disobeying God, they were expelled from Eden. God prohibited them from eating from the Tree of Life in order to prevent them from living forever in their fallen condition. This would have been an even worse judgment. The cherubim and the flame of a sword henceforth guarded the Tree of Life (Gen. 3:1–24).

Ever since that time, all men are forbidden to partake of the Tree of Life in their state of sin. There are a few notable exceptions to this situation, however. Enoch's fellowship with God led to his bodily translation, and Elijah was taken up to heaven in a whirlwind. Neither of them passed through death. God called Himself the God of Abraham, Isaac, and Jacob, several hundred years after their departure, implying that these three were really alive. The belief existed that the life in fellowship with God could not end or be broken even by death itself.

All of this changed at the coming of Jesus Christ, the Second Adam, who offers eternal life to all who believe in Him (1 John 5:11–12). The New Testament clearly teaches that zoe (Greek for "life") is available through Jesus Christ the Mediator. Jesus clearly taught that eternal life is a present possession as well as a future hope. Eternal life can be entered upon in this life through faith in Him.

Life, according to Jesus, has a duality about it. It is both quantitative and qualitative. It is temporal and eternal in terms of quantity. It can be abundant or deficient in regard to quality. Jesus is the Giver of life, the Sustainer of life, and the One whose presence or absence determines its quality. He is the "life force." He said, *"I have come that* [you] *may have life, and that* [you] *may have it more abundantly"* (John 10:10 NKJV).

Jesus openly claimed that He is *"the way, and the truth, and the life"* (John 14:6). He said, *"He who eats My flesh and drinks My blood has eternal life, and I will raise him up on the last day"* (John 6:54). *"And everyone who lives and believes in Me shall never die"* (John 11:26). Jesus is the spiritual fulfillment of the Tree of Life.

[3] The Westminister Shorter Catechism, 1647.

[4] A good source for further study on this subject is Mark and Patti Virkler, *Spirit-Born Creativity: Releasing God's Creativity into Your World* (Shippensburg, PA: Destiny Image Publishers, Inc., 1990).

[5] See chapter two, under the subhead "I Am the Problem."

Chapter Five: A Holy Spirit Explosion

[1] Rick Joyner has an excellent booklet entitled *Overcoming the Religious Spirit*, in which he addresses the issues of how to discern the religious spirit, and how it masks itself in the church today. He lists twenty-five warning signs of a religious spirit, then concludes with some practical steps on how to get rid of a religious spirit. See Rick Joyner, *Overcoming the Religious Spirit* (Charlotte, NC: MorningStar Publications, 1996). Also see Tommy Tenney, *God's Favorite House* (Shippensburg, PA: Destiny Image Publishers, Inc., 1999).

[2] Suggested reading:

> Lamar Boschman, *The Rebirth of Music* (Shippensburg, PA: Destiny Image Publishers, Inc., 1980).
>
> Joseph Garlington, *Worship: The Pattern of Things in Heaven* (Shippensburg, PA: Destiny Image Publishers, Inc., 1997).
>
> Robert Gay, *Silencing the Enemy* (Lake Mary, FL: Creation House, 1993).

Chapter Six: A New Level of Prayer

[1] Suggested reading:

> Edward W. Patton, *The Way into the Holiest* (New York: Thomas Nelson, 1983).
>
> C. W. Slemming, *Made according to Pattern* (Fort Washington, PA: Christian Literature Crusade, 1974).
>
> C. W. Slemming, *These Are the Garments* (Fort Washington, PA: Christian Literature Crusade, 1974).
>
> C. W. Slemming, *Thus Shalt Thou Serve* (Fort Washington, PA: Christian Literature Crusade, 1974).

[2] Suggested reading:

> Bob Sorge, *In His Face: A Prophetic Call to Renewed Focus* (Canandaigua, NY: Oasis House, 1994).

Part Two: The Well of His Presence

Chapter Seven: Come to the Well

[1] Mark Virkler categorizes five types of vision. One of these he refers to as a "spontaneous, unsought inner picture." This kind of vision is unsolicited, appearing out of nowhere. It is gentle and can be seen only with the eyes of the spirit. In his opinion, most Christians experience this type of vision. He cautions that we must test this, and all other types of vision, by the Scriptures. See Mark Virkler, *Dialogue with God* (South Plainfield, NJ: Bridge-Logos Publishing, 1986), 54–55.

[2] Prophets are people of vision. The Old Testament prophets occupy a significant place in the New Testament. T. Austin Sparks writes,

> They are the "seers" (1 Sam. 9:9); they are the men who see and, in seeing, act as eyes for the people of God. They are the men of vision; and their large place in the New Testament surely therefore indicates how tremendously important spiritual vision is for the people of God throughout this dispensation. Of course, the other thing is the vision itself....I feel the Lord is concerned with this factor—the tremendous importance of spiritual vision if the people of God are to fulfill their vocation. [See T. Austin Sparks, *Prophetic Ministry* (Shippensburg, PA: Destiny Image Publishers, Inc., 2000), 26.]

[3] Many different types of wells are mentioned in the Bible. They include cisterns dug in the ground (2 Sam. 17:17–19), springs (Ps. 84:6), fountains (Neh. 2:14 KJV), and pits or holes (John 4:5–6).

The actual process of digging a well in the days of Isaac (Gen. 26:18–22) and Uzziah (2 Chron. 26:10) was very difficult. Only crude tools were available, and sometimes it was necessary to dig a well to a great depth. Experts claim that Jacob's well was 150 feet deep. These deep wells were necessary because shallow wells would run dry during the long, rainless summers. Even in the most favorable locations, the water in Israel almost disappeared during the dry season.

The openings of these desert wells were always covered to protect the water. I was astounded to discover in my research that these wells were built so that they tapered to a narrow opening at the top, allowing for easy closure. Without any prior knowledge, I saw in the vision of the well of His presence a desert well exactly like those dug in the Eastern desert.

⁴ See Genesis 32:22–32. It is insightful to note the location where Jacob's wrestling with God took place—Jabbok (which means, "pouring out or river"), and Peniel (which means, "the face of God"). After Jacob crossed the place of "pouring out," he saw "the face of God."

⁵ Much to my amazement, as I researched the word *well* in the Old Testament, I discovered that one of its meanings is directly related to vision. When it occurs as *ayin*, it literally means "eye, well, surface, or appearance." It refers to a spring or an "eye" of water.

Ayin is also used to represent the bodily part, "eye," in Genesis 13:10. It is further connected with the expression of "seeing" in Genesis 45:12. Genesis 39:7 describes the lifting up of one's eyes (*ayin*) as an act of devotion, desire, or longing. This etymology adds even greater significance to the phrase *the well of His presence*. [See James Strong, *Strong's Exhaustive Concordance of the Bible* (Peabody, MA: Hendrickson Publishers), #5869.]

⁶ A great source for further study is Burton W. Seavey, *Christian Meditation: Doorway to the Spirit* (Buffalo, NY: IJN Publishing, 1988). See especially chapter six, "Looking into the Mysteries."

⁷ John Sanford has written an excellent book that deals with the inner meaning of Jesus' teachings. In his introduction titled, "The Old Well," he compares the sayings of Jesus to a rope that enables us to connect to our inner selves, and consequently to God. See John A. Sanford, *The Kingdom Within: The Inner Meaning of Jesus' Sayings* (New York: Paulist Press, 1970).

⁸ The words of Rick Joyner echo this thought: "A single word from God is worth more than all the treasure on earth!" See Rick Joyner, *The Call* (New Kensington, PA: Whitaker House, 1999) 179.

⁹ See Rick Joyner, *The Final Quest* (New Kensington, PA: Whitaker House, 1996), 9–12.

¹⁰ See Burton W. Seavey, *Christian Meditation: Doorway to the Spirit* (Buffalo, NY: IJN Publishing, 1988), chapter 13, "The Mystical Quality of Believers."

Chapter Eight: Choose Intimacy

¹ Compare with I Timothy 2:9–10; I Peter 3:3–4; I Corinthians 11:27, 34; James 1:21–25.

² *Dunamis* is one of the Greek words for power. It means ability or might. It is used to refer to miracles and mighty works or deeds. Our modern word *dynamite* is derived from it. See W. E. Vine, *Expository Dictionary of New Testament Words* (Old Tappan, NJ: Fleming H. Revell Company, 1966), 196.

[3] There are several excellent resources for more study on personal cleansing and intimacy with God:

> Cindy Jacobs, *Possessing the Gates of the Enemy: A Training Manual for Militant Intercession* (Tarrytown, NY: Chosen Books, Fleming H. Revell Company, 1991), 40.
>
> J. Oswald Sanders, *Enjoying Intimacy with God* (Chicago IL: Moody Press, 1980), 41.

Chapter Nine: Walking with Jesus

[1] In Amos 9:6 the prophet Amos spoke of God building His layers in the sky. The Hebrew word for layers, *ma'alah,* means "steps, stairs, upper chambers, ascents, or lofts." (Strong's #4609)

Chapter Ten: The Forest of Deception

[1] In these dynamic days of the fulfillment of God's purposes, countless numbers of Christians are being drawn to a deeper level of intimacy with the Lord. The Holy Spirit is calling us to come close to the living God, to seek His face, and to open our hearts to hear His voice.

We are living in a spiritual time warp, so to speak. Heaven and earth are commingling. Angels are appearing on a regular basis. Even encounters with the saints who have already passed into the heavenly realm are not out of the question. These things should not shock us. This very thing happened on the Mount of Transfiguration when Peter, James, and John witnessed the miraculous appearance of Moses and Elijah.

The Bible records that on the day that Jesus was crucified, many saints rose from the grave and made an appearance in the Holy City.

> *Jesus cried out again with a loud voice, and yielded up His spirit. And behold, the veil of the temple was torn in two from top to bottom, and the earth shook; and the rocks were split, and the tombs were opened; and many bodies of the saints who had fallen asleep were raised; and coming out of the tombs after His resurrection they entered the holy city and appeared to many.* (Matthew 27:50–53)

Imagine it! These people were actually seen walking through the streets of Jerusalem. Friends and family recognized them. Word rapidly spread through the city regarding their appearance.

I am, in no way, suggesting that we should seek such experiences, but on the other hand, why should we consider such occurrences suspect? Our God is the God of the living, not of the dead.

Chapter Eleven: The Living Word

[1] The phrase *word of the Lord* occurs in thirty-four books of the Bible. See Genesis 15:1; Exodus 9:20; Numbers 3:16; I Samuel 3:7; 15:10.

[2] In his treatise on the ministry of God's Word, Watchman Nee insightfully described the relationship between the Word of God and the human channel through which it is expressed. See Watchman Nee, *The Ministry of God's Word* (New York: Christian Fellowship Publishers, 1971), 26, 28.

[3] Most Bible students are familiar with the concepts relating to the Greek words *logos* and *rhema*. In my search to understand what I was experiencing on this occasion, I discovered an obscure third option used to express the meaning of "word." This alternate meaning is expressed by the Greek word *epos*.

Epos, "a word," is used in a phrase in Hebrews 7:9: literally "[as to say] a word"; "so to say," RV; "as I may so say," KJV. *Logos* is reasoned speech; *rhema*, an utterance; *epos*, the articulated expression of a thought. (See Abbot Smith, *International Standard Bible Encyclopedia*.)

Epos is used to describe the actual act of communicating. It is the process of dialogue, in which the word is experienced. This articulated expression of thought can occur only in the context of communion or intimacy. One must be in the presence of the person who is speaking in order to experience an *epos* word. This sheds light on the phrase, *the word of His presence,* or, *the proceeding word* that issues from Him in the moment of communication.

There are moments in life in which we are with those we love and have known for a long time, when words are not even necessary. The act of communicating occurs purely as a result of the intimacy that has developed over the years.

[4] The Word became flesh and dwelt among us in the incarnation of Jesus. He brought the Word of God from the realm of the spiritual into the realm of the flesh. He gave it a human savor. He made it available to our human senses of sight, touch, and hearing (John 1:1, 14). The Word (Jesus) dwells among men. Though the Word is indeed heavenly, nevertheless, it is not in heaven but on earth. Though intensely spiritual, it is definitely manifested in human form.

Chapter Twelve: The Book of Remembrance

[1] Elijah assumed the traditional posture of childbirth as he prayed for the drought to end. See also Galatians 4:19.

Chapter Thirteen: The Bride

[1] See chapter 1, under the subhead "On Angels' Wings."

Chapter Fourteen: The Throne Room

[1] Refer to chapter 6.

About the Author

D
r. Dale Arthur Fife is a gifted pastor, author, teacher, and musician, with an insatiable passion for intimacy with God. His zeal for the Lord has led him on an incredible journey from his first pastorate of a small rural church in a coal-mining town outside of Johnstown, Pennsylvania, to the cofounding of a large multiracial, inner-city church in Pittsburgh. After four decades of experience in ministry, he is now the senior pastor of a vibrant congregation in New England.

Whether leading worship for the first outdoor Jesus Festivals—as he did in the mid-seventies—or speaking in churches, conferences, and men's and women's gatherings for leaders or intercessors—as he does today—Dale's enthusiasm and hunger for God have always been contagious. His wisdom, maturity, and genuine spiritual concern for others have caused many to regard him as a "spiritual father" in the Lord. His insightful teaching has inspired and blessed thousands around the world.

Dr. Fife and his wife, Eunice, were married in 1963 and have two sons and six grandchildren. Dale graduated summa cum laude from the University of Pittsburgh. He completed seminary studies at Boston University School of Theology and did graduate study at Pittsburgh Theological Seminary. His doctor of divinity degree was conferred upon him by New Life College in Bangalore, India.

Since 1988, Dale and Eunice have served as senior pastors of The Potter's House International Worship and Training Center in Farmington, Connecticut. Dale and Eunice also serve on the board of directors of The Connecticut House of Prayer and Antioch International Ministries. They are the founders of Mountain Top Ministries, a network of pastors and leaders with local, regional, and international impact. The Fifes travel throughout the world, encouraging the body of Christ to passionately pursue God's presence and proclaiming the good news of God's hidden kingdom.

Dr. Fife is available for speaking engagements upon request. He may be reached at MnTopMin@aol.com for information regarding resources, itinerary, or to schedule ministry outreaches.

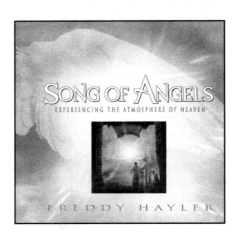

Song of Angels
Freddy Hayler

You have such a deep yearning for more of God, and your
heart desperately longs for His manifest presence. You just want
more. As you search for your place in His presence and as you
experience the *Song of Angels,* the message will intensify your
desire for a genuine visitation from God and will carry you to a
new dimension of intimacy with the Father.

ISBN: 0-88368-664-3 • Gift Book w/CD • 108 pages

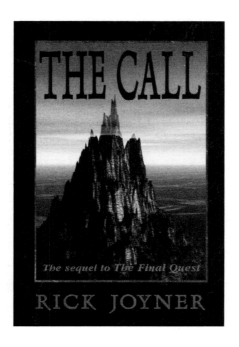

The Call
Rick Joyner

This compelling sequel to *The Final Quest* calls believers to seize the great spiritual opportunities available to us in these last days. *The Call* is a call to life, a call to live in the unprecedented glory of the Son of God, a call to sacrifice to do all things for the sake of the Gospel. Now is the time for Christians to take a stand against the darkness of our times for the sake of the Light who is surely coming.

ISBN: 0-88368-602-3 • Trade • 224 pages

WHITAKER HOUSE
Flooding the World with the Gospel
Visit our website at: www.whitakerhouse.com

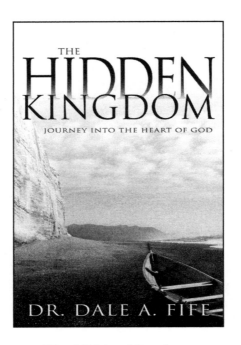

The Hidden Kingdom:
Journey into the Heart of God
Dr. Dale A. Fife

There are divine moments in life when you turn a corner
and are astounded by unexpected, breathtaking vistas that you
never imagined. Suddenly your world is changed forever. You
have entered a supernatural realm, an eternal dimension,
where Jesus is Lord and creation itself shouts His glory.
The brilliantly illuminating revelation in *The Hidden Kingdom*
will catapult you into such an experience. If you want
an empowered life, this book will lead you on a
journey into the heart of God.

ISBN: 0-88368-947-2 • Trade • 256 pages

WHITAKER HOUSE

Flooding the World with the Gospel
Visit our website at: www.whitakerhouse.com